THE STORY OF
Lee's Headquarters

GETTYSBURG, PENNSYLVANIA

by
Timothy H. Smith

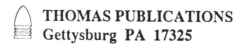

THOMAS PUBLICATIONS
Gettysburg PA 17325

Copyright © 1995 Timothy H. Smith

Printed and bound in the United States of America

Published by THOMAS PUBLICATIONS, P.O. Box 3031, Gettysburg, Pa. 17325

ISBN-0-939631-85-7

Cover design by Ryan C. Stouch

Contents

Preface

When at first I began to research this project, I discovered that the story of Lee's headquarters has many elements. Some are well documented facts, some are conjecture, and some are down right fiction. When I began to solicit help from my fellow guides and historians, I realized that many of them were just as, if not more, confused as I was. Much of what we know about Mary Thompson, the resident of the stone house on Seminary Ridge at the time of the battle, is based on myth and oral history (see page 215 of Glenn Tucker's *High Tide At Gettysburg* for example). Sorting out fact from myth and finding documentation to support these long told legends concerning the "Widow Thompson" and her stone house quickly became my major concern.

But beyond the story of the house and its use as the headquarters of General Lee there was another story to be told. The terrific fighting that took place on Seminary Ridge on the afternoon of July 1, 1863 has long been ignored by historians. Although I did not initially intend on delving into this aspect of the Thompson House, the result is probably the most accurate and extensive coverage of this portion of the battle to date. Many individuals and organizations were responsible in aiding me in my endeavor to present this study in its final form. I would like to extend my most heartfelt thanks to the following individuals.

First and foremost on my list is Andrew M. Larson, former owner of General Lee's Headquarters Museum (GLHM), without whose support and encouragement this book certainly would have never been written. It has always been his vision that the story of Mary Thompson and the struggle around her house be told.

The Adams County Historical Society (ACHS) by far was the most beneficial source of information that I came in contact with during my research. Their resources are unsurpassed, in quantity and quality, when one is researching the life of an Adams County resident. Their staff was always courteous, and the many conversations that I had with its director, Charles H. Glatfelter, and research historian Elwood W. Christ were most enlightening. It was there that I read the only other manuscript I have ever seen dealing with this subject, "Where Were Lee's Headquarters During the Battle of Gettysburg, July 1st, 2nd, and 3rd, 1863?" written by Jeffrey L. Patterson in 1982. This manuscript along with subsequent conversations held with Jeff, greatly added to my comprehension of the early history of the Thompson House.

It was also through the society's files that I was able to make contact with several direct descendants of Mary Thompson including R. William Bean of Urbana, Ohio, (descendant of Elias Thompson) with whom I conversed over the phone on countless evenings, discussing information and leads concerning Mary's family history. Evelyn D. Hughes of Lewisberry, Pennsylvania shared with me a wealth of knowledge concerning her great grandmother, Hannah Phillipina Sell

Foulk. Pauline Pheneger of Ohio, and Amy Hutton of West Palm Beach, Florida also gave me information that was vital to the finished product.

I would also like to extend my thanks the staff of the Gettysburg National Military Park (GNMP), the United States Army Military History Institute (USAMHI) at Carlisle Barracks, and the National Archives (NA) in Washington, D.C., for their help in locating several pieces of rare source material. The staff at Thomas Publications was most helpful in preparing the final manuscript.

And of course, a big thanks must go to my colleagues and friends in the Association of Licensed Battlefield Guides (ALBG). Unbeknownst to most of them at the time, the entire guide force has helped me in one way or another through argument or discussion in discovering sources of information that were valuable in my research. I am very fortunate to be a part of such an unique group of men and women. Most notably on this project were the assistance of James Clouse and Howard Koser, who read over the original manuscript and made many valuable corrections or suggestions; and, David L. Richards, Wayne E. Motts, Charles Fennell, Tim Krapf, Gregory Coco, Edward Guy, and Louise Arnold Friend, who all at one time or another helped out with portions of the text. I would also like to thank a few of the people who were responsible in helping develop my deep interest in history, including my late father, Howard James Smith, and my good friends, Robert Williamson, Steve Doyle, Pete Nicholas, Richard Adams, and Jeff Stansbury.

A special thanks must go to the following individuals for their help on this as well as other projects. First, my good friend and mentor William A. Frassanito, who was always quick with encouragement or suggestions on any topic I might be interested in. Secondly, my friend and fellow Licensed Battlefield Guide Garry Adelman, whose original and innovative maps are without equal in detail and accuracy. I am very fortunate that they are introduced here in print for the first time anywhere. Finally, I must acknowledge the support given to me by my family and especially my wife Diane, without whose patience and understanding this work could never have been completed. She read and reread copy after copy of my manuscript in different stages of production and made revisions on my spelling and grammar in every version. All of these people and many more were responsible in helping me to document the story that will be told on the following pages.

Timothy H. Smith
Gettysburg, PA

THE STORY OF
Lee's Headquarters

GETTYSBURG, PENNSYLVANIA

Aerial view of Seminary Ridge taken in 1969. Surrounded by modern development, the Thompson House can be seen along the Chambersburg Pike, just west of what was then the Dutch Pantry (now JD's Grill). Walter Lane Collection, ACHS.

Introduction

On the crest of Seminary Ridge, along the north side of the Chambersburg Turnpike, stands a one and a half story stone dwelling used as a museum and known today as General Lee's Headquarters. Surrounded by modern development, it is easy to forget the importance that this building held in 1863. Around it, however, some of the bloodiest and most desperate fighting of the Battle of Gettysburg was waged. At the time of the Civil War, the house was owned by Thaddeus Stevens, a Republican Congressman from Pennsylvania, who had purchased the house in 1846 at a sheriff's auction "in trust" for Mary Thompson. In July 1863, Mary was 69 years old, widowed, and living alone. Much of the fascination with the stone house on Seminary Ridge revolves around this "Widow Thompson." Who was she, who was her late husband, and what was her relationship to Thaddeus Stevens? These are questions which have never been properly answered.

During the battle, the ridge on which the Thompson house stood was occupied by Union artillery and used as a Northern defensive position. It was attacked by Confederate infantry and captured by force. Seminary Ridge was then converted into a Southern defensive position and occupied by Confederate artillery, and, because of its critical location in the middle of the Southern lines, and adjacent to the Chambersburg Pike, it also became the perfect place for General Robert Edward Lee to establish his headquarters. No other position on the battlefield can make such a distinctive claim. Over the years, many people have questioned the validity of this assertion, and while it is not the author's intention to suggest that the Thompson House was Lee's one and only headquarters during the battle, evidence will be presented that places him in the structure. Evidence will also be presented, much of it for the first time, to show the magnitude of the terrible fighting that took place around the house. In the years since the Civil War, Mrs. Thompson and her stone house have become enshrined in the history and lore of the Battle of Gettysburg every bit as much as the men who actually fought there. Her story, and that of the desperate struggle around her house, deserves to be told.

PART
I

Early History

In 1681, William Penn received a grant from Charles II of England for 45,000 square miles of land. Today that land is known as Pennsylvania or "Penn's Woods." The ground around which the Thompson House now stands was originally called Marsh Creek Settlement, and was first established by Scotch-Irish immigrants in the 1730s.[1] In 1741 the area became part of the "Manor of Maske," a 43,500 acre tract of land set aside by John, Richard, and Thomas Penn (the sons of William). On May 30, 1765, a warrant was issued by the Penn family to Robert Stewart for 121 acres of ground in Cumberland Township, York County. Sometime prior to 1773, the tract was conveyed to William Breaden, who in turn transferred the tract to Reverend David McConaughy on October 18, 1802.[2]

In 1800, Adams County was formed out of the western part of York County and named for John Adams, the President of the United States. A crossroads town situated in the center of the county was chosen as its seat. At a sheriff's auction in 1785, the enterprising James Gettys had purchased 116 acres of land around what was then a major intersection, laid out 210 lots, and in January 1786, established the town now known as Gettysburg.[3] As the new county seat, the town quickly expanded, and the necessity soon arose for new roads to connect it with all parts of the county. In 1812 the Gettysburg and Petersburg Turnpike Company started construction on a toll road west from the town that ran directly across Reverend McConaughy's property. Fifty-one years later, this road (the Chambersburg Pike) played a major role in leading the Southern army to the small crossroads town of Gettysburg.[4]

On March 8, 1827, McConaughy transferred his property to David Ziegler, Michael C. Clarkson, and John Fuller. In 1832, Clarkson bought out his other two partners and established sole ownership of the property.[5] It was under his ownership that the stone house we see today on Seminary ridge was built. While the inscription "1779" is carved on a stone at the base of the Thompson House, there is no documentation to suggest the house is that old. In fact, the evidence is very much to the contrary. It is not known whether Clarkson or any member of his family ever lived in the dwelling, but it does appear that the house was built in 1833, or 1834, while the property was under his ownership.[6]

Michael C. Clarkson had moved to Gettysburg in 1822 from Lancaster, Pennsylvania, where his father was a Lutheran minister.[7] On September 5 of that

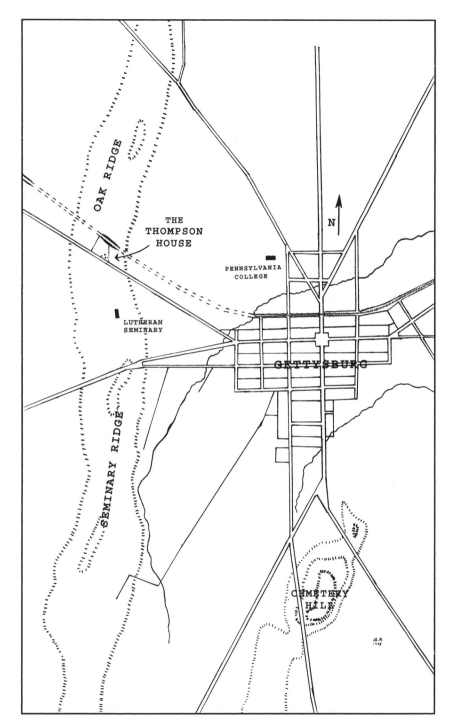

The Thompson House in relationship to the town of Gettysburg.

same year he was married to Louisa Harper by the Reverend David McConaughy.[8] Clarkson, who would eventually own several pieces of property in and around town, became a prominent figure in Gettysburg, serving on the town council in 1832 and 1842, as town burgess in 1837 and 1839, and as owner of a dry goods business situated on the corner of Baltimore and Middle Streets.[9]

Although Michael Clarkson was a renowned businessman in his own right, it is probably his strong political allegiance to Thaddeus Stevens for which he is best remembered today. Stevens, who is better known as a "Radical Republican" for his views on Reconstruction after the Civil War, was a key player in early Gettysburg politics, and "by the time he left for Lancaster in the summer of 1842, in search of larger opportunities, there were few aspects of Adams County life which he had not influenced in some major way."[10]

In 1837 Clarkson was appointed Superintendent of the Gettysburg extension of the Pennsylvania Railroad, better known as the "Tapeworm Railroad," not only because of the route, which wound its way through the South Mountains, but also because of the way it ate up taxpayers' money. Many people believed that this project was no more than a scheme, orchestrated by the wealthy and powerful Thaddeus Stevens, to build a railway from his iron works at Maria Furnace to the Baltimore and Ohio railroad in Maryland, at the expense of the people of Pennsylvania. There are also accounts to suggest that Clarkson abused his job as superintendent, and allegations were made that he forced employees to vote only for candidates in support of the railroad's construction. In April 1839, the Pennsylvania Legislature launched an investigation into the railway, the work was terminated, Clarkson lost his job, and the unfinished railroad was left abandoned.[11]

Along some stretches of the route however, construction had almost been completed. Land was filled, streams were forded, and cuts had been made through ridges to level out a bed for which the tracks could be laid. Ironically, part of the railroad ran directly across Clarkson's property west of town, and a huge cut had to be carved through Seminary Ridge just a few yards north of the newly built stone house.[12] Much of the dirt taken from this cut was then used to build up an embankment across the low ground leading into town. For years afterward, it became common practice for townspeople to use the unfinished railroad bed as a road and thereby avoid paying the toll on the Chambersburg Pike.[13] During the first day of the Battle of Gettysburg this deep railroad cut near the Thompson House became a trap for the men of the retreating Northern army, and for many, their ticket to a Southern prison. Today, although the names are commonly interchanged, the railroad cut is the imaginary dividing line between Oak Ridge and Seminary Ridge.

During their marriage Clarkson's wife gave birth to at least 10 children, one of whom, born in 1840, was named Thaddeus Stevens Clarkson in honor of their good friend.[14] The same year, Clarkson fell into financial trouble when he defaulted on a note for $1,800. Legal proceedings in Adams County Court led to a sheriff's auction of his properties, and in August 1844, notice was served on Clarkson's wife and on a tenant of Clarkson's, Mary Thompson.[15] At some point, three acres which included the Thompson House were divided from Clarkson's original tract along

An 1843 woodcut of Gettysburg from the west. The wagon in the foreground is shown riding eastward into town on the bed of the unfinished "Tapeworm Railroad." ACHS.

Seminary Ridge, and this, along with other properties he owned, were put up for sale. At the auction, held in January 1846, the stone house and the three acres of land were purchased by Thaddeus Stevens as a trustee of Mary Thompson.[16]

> To Thaddeus Stevens for No. 3 a lot of ground adjoining tract No. 2 and lands of Thaddeus Stevens and others containing three acres more or less on which are erected a one and one half story stone dwelling house and frame stable—which Benjamin Schriver esquire High Sheriff of the County of Adams has seized by virtue of a writ of alias *bendetioni expouos*, to him for that purpose directed and sold and struck off the same unto Thaddeus Stevens, trustee of Mary Thompson, for the sum of sixteen dollars—Deed dated Jan. 28, 1846.
>
> I hereby acknowledge that Thaddeus Stevens, who purchased the property described in the within deed, the same in trust for me only so far as he has received money to which I am entitled. Witness my hand and seal the 4 day of February, 1846. Mary x (her mark) Thompson. Witness, James A. Thompson and Benjamin Schriver.[17]

The information we have concerning Mary's life is very sketchy, and little is known of her early years. She was born near Littlestown, Pennsylvania, on November 12, 1793, under the name of Ann Marie Long. She was the daughter of Philip Leopold and Phillipina Long (or Lang).[18] About 1818, she married a man named Daniel Sell, and soon after gave birth to a child named Eliza. In the 1820 Adams County Census, Daniel Sell is listed as living in Germany Township with his wife, and their newly born child.[19] The family later moved to Maryland, where, on February 11, 1821, Mary gave birth to a second daughter. She was named Hannah Phillipina Sell and was baptized in September of that year.[20]

Tragedy struck Mary's family in the fall of 1822, when her husband Daniel, only 30 years of age, suddenly died.[21] Moving back to Pennsylvania, the "Widow Sell" gave birth to a third daughter, Mary Jane, on January 19, 1823.[22] It is not known exactly where Mary lived while she was a widow, but she did not remain single for long. By the fall of 1826 she was remarried to a man named Joshua F. Thompson.[23] Again there is very little documentation concerning the life of Joshua, Mary's second husband, but it is believed he was born in Pennsylvania about 1805.[24] On June 19, 1827, their union produced Mary's first son, James Henry Thompson.[25] On December 25, 1828, she gave birth to a second son, Elias Thompson.[26] In 1830 Joshua and his family moved to Franklin Township, Adams County, onto a farm along the "Hunterstown Road" owned by Philip Long.[27] In the 1830 Adams County Census, Joshua Thompson, between 20 and 30 years of age, is shown living with a female between 30 and 40 (Mary), two males under 5 (James and Elias), and two females between 5 and 10 (Eliza and Mary Jane).[28]

During the 1830s the Thompson family worked their Franklin Township farm, owning no more than a few cows and horses each year.[29] During these years Mary gave birth to three more children, Catherine Sarah on November 25, 1830, Margaret Isabella on June 21, 1834, and Susannah Long Thompson in 1836.[30] Joshua's occupation was listed as "choper," but times were hard, and it must have been difficult to support his family.[31] Consequently he began to drink quite heavily, and in 1836 disappears from the tax records, apparently leaving his family. The next year, three of the Thompson children appear on the list of Poor Children for Franklin Township.[32] In February 1838 Mary received $250 from the estate of her late father, and Joshua's name reappears in the records. But again in 1839 his name disappears from the records, this time, never to return.[33]

It seems that his problems became too much for him to handle, and at some point Joshua completely abandoned his family. In the 1840 Adams County Cen-

Mary Thompson (1793-1873). This photo has been on continuous display at General Lee's Headquarters Museum since the early 1920's. GLHM.

sus the name Joshua Thompson is not found, but Mary Thompson is listed in Menallen Township, with what appears to be four of her children.[34] In November of 1841 Mary's oldest child, Eliza Sell, appeared before the Adams County Court of Common Pleas, and petitioned that her stepfather be declared a "habitual drunkard," stating that he had been one for the last eight years and "by reason there of" was "rendered altogether unfit to govern himself and manage his affairs."[35] An inquest was held at the home of James Heagy in Gettysburg, on December 11, 1841, to decide the issue.

> William N. Irvine and the solemn oaths and affirmations of James Major, Robert King, Ephraim Martin, Samuel H. Buehler, Bernhart Gilbert, and Daniel Baldwin, six good, honest, and lawful men of the said County, who being respectively sworn or affirmed to inquire of the premises on their oaths and affirmations do say—That the said Joshua Thompson is at the time of taking this Inquisition and Habitual Drunkard so that he is not capable of the government of himself, his manner—messuages, Tenements, goods and Chattels and that he hath been an habitual drunkard for the space of ten years last past.[36]

It is not known where Joshua Thompson was living at the date of the inquest, and at the present time his whereabouts cannot be determined for certain after the year 1838. He seems to disappear, and or leave town, apparently dying sometime prior to March 1850.[37] Just a few days after the inquest Mary filed a petition stating that because "her said husband has been found an Habitual Drunkard," her children "under the age of fourteen...have no guardian, and as her said husband is...disqualified and incompetent to act as such," she asked that someone else be appointed for that purpose. On the original petition the name Thaddeus Stevens was given as the preferred guardian, but his name was crossed out and David Ziegler's name was written above it. James Henry Thompson, who was fourteen at the time, filed a separate petition also naming Ziegler as his guardian. Both petitions were approved and David Ziegler became the guardian of all five Thompson children.[38] At some point prior to 1844, Mary and her family moved to Cumberland Township and became residents of Michael Clarkson's stone house on Seminary Ridge. Considering that David Ziegler, the guardian of the Thompson children, had been one of Clarkson's partners in the original purchase of the property in 1827, and that Thaddeus Stevens was involved, it is no coincidence that Mary's family ended up in that particular house.[39]

At the auction of Clarkson's properties in January 1846, Thaddeus Stevens bought the tract which included the stone house, "in trust" for Mary Thompson for just $16.[40] The speculation regarding the relationship between Mrs. Thompson and Thaddeus Stevens has been plentiful, and sometimes a bit melodramatic, but much of it stems from the fact that Stevens somehow managed to buy the stone house and lot for such an insignificant sum.[41] It may be that Stevens bought the house as a trustee for Mary because her husband was still alive, and the fear existed that he might return to Gettysburg and take the property from her. At that time (1846) a married woman could not legally hold title to property in the state of Pennsylvania.[42]

This fear was alleviated however, with the death of Joshua Thompson sometime before March 1850. In a letter sent from Washington D.C. on March 9, of that year, Thaddeus Stevens informed Mrs. Thompson that "the amount of money which according to contract with your late husband I had for your use was ($360) three hundred and sixty dollars. That would leave a deficiency of $140 at the time of the original purchase." Stevens also mentioned that he would be in town "sometime the last of April the first of May" to discuss the situation with her.[43] It seems that Stevens had some sort of contract with Mary's husband before he died, and had owed him money. At the auction he had bought the property on her behalf for $16, but was charging her $500 for it. There may be a simple explanation for what transpired, such as Stevens paying off another of Clarkson's debts and the sheriff subtracting the total from the price of the house. So much time has now passed since the events surrounding the auction that historians may never know the real story.

All this leads to the question of who actually did hold title to the Thompson House at the time of the battle? As early as 1851 Mrs. Thompson is shown in the Cumberland Township tax records as the owner of the property, and is listed as such up to, and beyond the time of her death. But as the $140 that Mary still apparently owed Thaddeus Stevens went unpaid, technically the property remained in his possession.[44]

The minutes of the board of directors of the Lutheran Theological Seminary record that in April of 1846 Mrs. Thompson was hired as their steward. In this position Mary probably cooked and did laundry for the students that were housed in the "Old Dorm" of the Lutheran Seminary. According to the records, she held the position for just a few years and by 1851 the board had named a new steward. It is possible, however, that she may have continued to perform odd jobs from time to time for some of the Seminary personnel.[45]

In the 1850 Adams County Census, Mary Thompson and her family are living in Cumberland Township. All eight of Mary's children are listed as living

Thaddeus Stevens (1792-1868). **ACHS.**

with her in the stone house on Seminary Ridge.[46] In the 1856 Cumberland Township Tax Records, Mary is described for the first time in a way for which she will always be remembered, simply as "Widow Thompson."[47]

As the years went by, her children, one by one, married, and moved away. By 1860, although a few of her children resided near by, the census shows that Mary was living alone.[48] Her oldest son, James Henry Thompson, his wife Mary, and their small child lived just across the pike, in a house which still stands today.[49] Hannah had married a blacksmith named Samuel K. Foulk, and was living in a house just a few hundred feet down the Chambersburg Pike from her mother. In 1860 Hannah was living with her husband, four children, and Cornelius Beecher, her husband's assistant.[50] Life around Gettysburg at this time must have seemed very pleasant. Little did anyone realize that events would soon occur to propel Mrs. Thompson and her stone house into the national press.

Hannah Phillipina Foulk (1821-1900).
Photo taken in 1899. **Courtesy of Evelyn D. Hughes.**

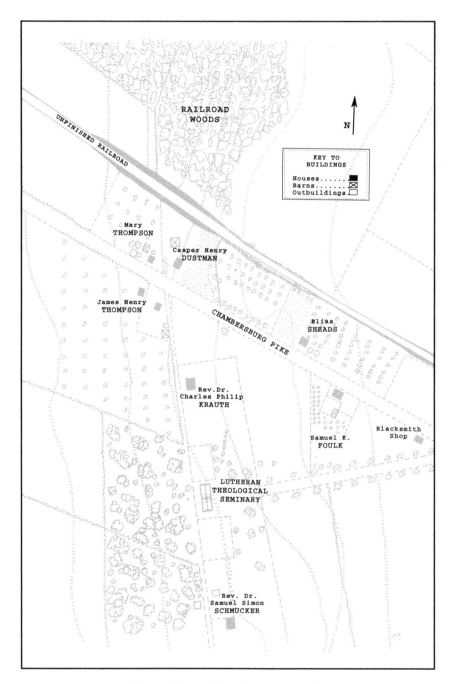

RAILROAD
WOODS

N

KEY TO
BUILDINGS
Houses......■
Barns.......⊠
Outbuildings□

UNFINISHED RAILROAD

Mary
THOMPSON

Casper Henry
DUSTMAN

James Henry
THOMPSON

CHAMBERSBURG PIKE

Elias
SHEADS

Rev.Dr.
Charles Philip
KRAUTH

Samuel K.
FOULK

Blacksmith
Shop

LUTHERAN
THEOLOGICAL
SEMINARY

Rev. Dr.
Samuel Simon
SCHMUCKER

The residences along Seminary Ridge.

PART
II

The War

With the outbreak of the American Civil War, Gettysburg, like many towns, was changed forever. Even though the war had not been officially carried into Pennsylvania during its first two years, it was still very much a part of the daily lives of Adams County civilians. With a population of about 2,400, many of the men and boys in and around Gettysburg joined the army, and fought for the cause they felt just, some of them very near neighbors of the Thompson's. John Henry Dustman, who lived right next door, enlisted with Company F of the 87th Pennsylvania, and Elias Sheads, who in 1862 built a house just across the Chambersburg Pike from that of Samuel and Hannah Foulk, gave four sons to the war effort. All four would die as a result of their service.[1] In November 1862, Mary's own son, James Henry Thompson enlisted as a substitute in Company H of the 165th Pennsylvania Infantry.[2] The 165th, made up mostly of men drafted from Adams County, were not present at the Battle of Gettysburg, being stationed in Suffolk, Virginia where they saw little action during their service. As a nine-month unit, their enlistment ran out on July 28, 1863, just three weeks after the battle.[3]

Throughout the years of 1861 and 1862, the citizens of Adams County were very concerned about their close proximity to the Mason-Dixon Line. There were frequent false alarms of "guerrilla raids" in the area, and "amateur scouts" would often ride into the town crying "the Rebels are coming!"[4] In October of 1862 a Confederate cavalry force under the command of the flamboyant Southern cavalryman J.E.B. Stuart, actually did pass through the western part of Adams County while on a raid through southern Pennsylvania, and it was reported that some of his troopers had come to within four miles of town.[5] But most of the people laughed at the prospect of the Confederates coming to such a small unimportant town as Gettysburg. It would not be until the summer of 1863 that a uniformed Southern soldier would enter its streets.

In June of 1863 Robert E. Lee's Army of Northern Virginia, more than 70,000 strong, crossed the Potomac River and made its advance into southern Pennsylvania. The invasion was a chance to take the war out of the devastated region of northern Virginia, whose farms were burdened with the task of feeding the two large armies that had been campaigning there for the past two years. As Lee's army moved through the towns and communities of the North, they also gathered supplies and provisions that were so desperately needed. With the Northern Army of the Potomac still in Virginia, and slow to respond to the invasion, Lee had a free hand in the wealthy farmlands of southern Pennsylvania. Governor Curtin called for

A wartime photo of James Henry Thompson (1827-1908) and his first wife, Mary Jane (Arendt) Thompson. **Courtesy of the descendants of James H. Thompson.**

volunteers to help defend the state capital, and emergency regiments were hastily formed. One of these regiments was sent to the crossroads of Gettysburg, and on June 26th, tried to confront the advance of General Jubal Early's 5,000 man division a few miles west of town. The 26th Pennsylvania Emergency Regiment, 743 men (Co. A being comprised of 83 men from Gettysburg) with less than a week of military experience, was no match for the battle-hardened veterans of Early's Division and were easily routed.[6] The Confederates marched right past the Thompson House and on into the square of town, where they made demands for sugar, coffee, flour, salt, bacon, onions, whiskey, shoes, hats, and $5,000 in cash.[7] It is not known how much of the ransom was made, but stores were opened and the Confederates searched the town for supplies. Most civilians recalled afterward that the Rebels "were generally civil," and some even tried to pay for the goods they procured with Confederate money. The raiders burned the railroad bridge east of town, and by the morning of June 27th, moved away from Gettysburg, marching toward a bigger objective, the city of York.[8]

By the end of June, Lee's forces were scattered all over the Pennsylvania countryside. Some of them had marched as far east as the town of Wrightsville, along the banks of the Susquehanna River. Some of Lee's force was as far north as Carlisle and the outskirts of Harrisburg, but most of his army was still about 26 miles west of Gettysburg, near the town of Chambersburg. On the evening of June 28th, Lee was informed that the Army of the Potomac was advancing northward very rapidly, and was now closing in on his position. Lee knew that the time had come to concentrate his forces and prepare for battle. The road hub at Gettysburg must have looked like a blessing in disguise; ten roads led into the town from virtually all the other towns in the area. It was the most logical place to concentrate his spread out army. In a letter written the day after the battle to Confederate President Jefferson Davis, Lee wrote that as soon as "intelligence was received that the army of General Hooker was advancing [his] whole force was directed to concentrate at Gettysburg."[9]

On June 30th, the Confederates again approached town from the west. Reaching the top of Seminary Ridge on the Chambersburg Pike, a group of officers from General James J. Pettigrew's North Carolina Brigade stopped in front of the Thompson House and watched as two brigades of Federal cavalry, under the command of Brigadier General John Buford, entered the previously undefended town from the south. Major General Henry Heth described that "Under these circumstances, he [Pettigrew] did not deem it advisable to enter the town," and retired his forces back in the direction of Cashtown. As a result, General Buford ordered his men to advance through the town and take up position in the fields west and north of it. The stage was now set for the bloodiest battle in American history.[10]

The Battle of Gettysburg began as a small clash of arms between two brigades of Northern cavalry under the command of General John Buford, and two brigades of Southern infantry under the command of Major General Henry Heth. Although there were scattered shots throughout the morning, the fighting did not begin until 8:00 a.m. Sarah Broadhead, who lived on Chambersburg Street at the western edge of town, described the events of July 1, 1863, in her diary.

> I got up early this morning to get my baking done before any fighting would begin. I had just put my bread in the pans when the cannons began to fire, and true enough the battle had begun in earnest, about two miles out on the Chambersburg Pike. What to do or where to go, I did not know. People were running here and there, screaming that the town would be shelled. No one knew where to go or what to do.[11]

During those early morning hours, many of the townspeople ventured out to Seminary Ridge to get a closer look at the fighting. Daniel Skelly was one of these young men. As he moved across the fields west of the town, he joined some others who were already positioned in the "Railroad Woods." As luck would have it, he watched the opening moments of the battle just a few yards north of the Thompson House.

> I remained on Seminary Ridge just where the "Old Tape-worm" railroad cuts through it. The ridge was full of men and boys from the town, all eager to witness a brush with the Confederates and not dreaming of the terrible conflict that was to occur on that day and not having the slightest conception of the proximity of the two armies. I climbed up a good-sized tree so as to have a good view of the ridge west and northwest of us, where the two brigades of cavalry were then being placed. We could then hear distinctly the skirmish fire in the vicinity of Marsh Creek, about three miles from our position and could tell that it was approaching nearer and nearer as our skirmishers fell back slowly toward the town contesting every inch of ground. We could see clearly on the ridge about a half mile beyond us, the formation of the line of battle of Buford's Cavalry, which had dismounted, some of the men taking charge of the horses and others forming a line of battle, acting as infantry.
>
> Nearer and nearer came the skirmish line as it fell back before the advancing Confederates, until at last the line on the ridge beyond became engaged. Soon the artillery opened fire and shot and shell began to fly over our heads, one of them passing dangerously near the top of the tree I was on. There was then a general stampede toward town and I quickly slipped down from my perch and joined the retreat to the rear of our gallant men and boys. I started for town on the "Old Tape-worm Railroad," but crossed from it over a field to the Chambersburg Pike on the east side of Miss Carrie Sheads' School and when about the middle of the field a cannon ball struck the earth about fifteen or twenty feet from me, scattering the ground somewhat about me and quickening my pace considerably.[12]

Years later, Catherine Foster, described the same scene as she and her family watched from the western balcony of their home on West High Street.

> ...[Our men] turned toward the town dashing and flying over fences and fields in every direction, like a shower of meteors. The artillery began to play and the shells to whiz over our heads. The students who had to the present time remained in the Seminary, as well as the occupants of the other buildings on the ridge, came running to town at a speed greater than double quick. Old Lady Thompson, however, at Lee's Headquarters, never deserted her house during the entire battle.[13]

Just after 10:00 a.m. the first infantry of the Army of the Potomac arrived on the field, and "the shells began to fly around quite thick."[14] Major General John Reynolds' First Army Corps arrived just in time to relieve Buford's weary cavalrymen and beat back the attack of Heth's surprised Confederates, who had not expected to meet up with Northern infantry that day. This initial engagement was a Union victory, but at a terrible cost. John Fulton Reynolds, one of the North's most capable generals, was shot from his horse and killed instantly, while leading the famous "Iron Brigade" into battle. As the day went on, more Union and Confederate troops continued to converge on the small crossroads town of Gettysburg, and the battle continued to grow in size. Before the three days of fighting were over, it would become the greatest battle ever fought on the North American continent.

By noon on July 1st, there was a lull in the fighting, both sides licking their wounds and preparing for the continuation of hostilities. As more Northern reinforcements arrived they were placed into position across the fields north and west of town. With the arrival of the Eleventh Corps of the Army of the Potomac, command of the field fell into the hands of Major General Oliver Otis Howard. General Howard resolved to hold out as long as he could, dispute every inch of ground, and wait for the arrival of Union reinforcements. But with Lee's entire force now concentrating on the town, more Southern troops were arriving every minute, from the west as well as from the north.

Sometime around 2:00 p.m. the cannons reopened, and the battle was renewed with the attack of General Robert Rodes' 8,000 man division arriving from the direction of Carlisle. Just as the fighting resumed, Robert E. Lee himself arrived on the field, and with the battle already underway north of town, he had no choice but to order General Heth to also continue his attack. With the added weight of Heth's two fresh brigades, the Union First Corps were soon forced from their advanced position on McPherson's Ridge. The Federal troops would rally one more time that day and make a final stand on Seminary Ridge, but it would just be a matter of time before the combined Confederate forces would outflank and overwhelm the outnumbered Union defenders. And the Thompson House would be right in the center of this final defensive position.

The Chambersburg Pike, the unfinished railroad cut, Seminary Ridge, and Oak Ridge, four of the most prominent land features on the first day's battlefield, all intersect within feet of Mary Thompson's stone house. As a result, some of the heaviest fighting of the battle would be done on and around her property. As the sounds of battle reawakened, Casper Henry Dustman, also a resident of Seminary Ridge, recalled that "the bullets and shells flew thick and fast, and they made such a queer sound going through the air."[15]

PART III

Pender's Attack

With the Federal retreat from McPherson's Ridge, and the Southerners sensing victory, the attack was renewed with increased fury. As the Northern infantrymen fell back toward the Seminary, "the hollow" between the two ridges "became hot with the incessant hum of the bees of battle."[1] Lieutenant Colonel Rufus Dawes of the 6th Wisconsin stood at the edge of the Railroad Woods, just north of the Thompson House, and watched as the Confederates surged "down the opposite slope under a cloud of fire and smoke."[2]

> Along the Seminary Ridge, flat upon their bellies, lay mixed up together in one line of battle the Iron Brigade and Roy Stone's "Bucktails." For a mile up and down the open fields before us the splendid lines of the veterans of the Army of Northern Virginia swept down upon us. Their bearing was magnificent. They maintained their alignments with great precision. In many cases the colors of regiments were advanced several paces in front of the line.[3]

The attacking columns referred to by Colonel Dawes were the three brigades of Major General Dorsey Pender's Division. These men had just relieved those of General Heth's, and were now launching an all out assault on the Federal position along Seminary Ridge. From right to left, the brigades of James Lane, Abner Perrin, and Alfred Scales, almost 5,000 battle hardened Rebels, were now bearing down upon the Union lines.

For the already battered troops of the Union First Corps, the sight of yet more Southern reinforcements must have looked very ominous indeed. But luckily for the Northern soldiers, there was an ace in the hole. The Union high command had seen the importance of Seminary Ridge as a final defensive position in the event their forces were driven off McPherson's Ridge, and throughout the day had been taking steps to fortify it. Hours earlier, the commander of the Union First Corps, Major General Abner Doubleday, had ordered his Second Division to "throw up some slight intrenchments" at the grove in front of the Seminary, and now these breastworks "weak and imperfect" as they were, became a rallying point for the soldiers preparing to receive the onslaught of Pender's fresh division. The men behind this "semi-circular entrenchment" were "lying down and firing over the rails" toward the advancing foe.[4]

The line of the Union First Corps now extended from a point near the Hagerstown Road, north through the Seminary, across the Chambersburg Pike, the railroad cut, and over Oak Ridge to the Mummasburg Road. Almost at right angles with the First Corps, and defending the fields north of the town, were the soldiers of the Eleventh Corps of the Army of the Potomac, but with the arrival of Jubal Early's 5,000 man division from the northeast, these soldiers had their hands full. Doubleday could expect no help from them nor from the division of reserves General Howard was holding on Cemetery Hill.

Of the 28 regiments (more than 9,000 men) the First Corps had present on the battlefield, every one of them had already been engaged in the fight. The losses had been high, and some units had been decimated. There were no reserves at hand, and none were coming. To make things worse, both flanks were about to be simultaneously attacked by fresh troops. It was about 4:00 p.m. and Doubleday recalled that "the enemy were now closing in on us from the south, west, and north, and still no orders came to retreat."[5] The infantry were going to need help if they were to hold their position. The task of placing artillery along this ridge was very important, and the responsibility fell into the capable hands of Colonel Charles S. Wainwright, commander of the First Corps artillery.

> The Cashtown road being our most important point, each one had aimed to take care of it. Robinson had ordered Stewart [Battery B, 4th U.S.] to take post on each side of the railroad. Doubleday had ordered Stevens [5th Maine Battery] from where I had placed him at the left to the road itself. Cooper [Battery B, 1st Pennsylvania] had his four guns immediately in front of the main building [The Lutheran Seminary], and Wilber's section [Battery L, 1st New York] came down the road with Wadsworth's division. Thus there were eighteen pieces on a frontage of not over two hundred yards.[6]

Just a few yards west of the Widow Thompson's house were the six Napoleons of Battery B, 4th United States Artillery under the direction of Lieutenant James Stewart. Three of the guns, under the command of Lieutenant James Davison, were positioned between the Chambersburg Pike and the railroad cut. The other three were positioned north of the cut in front of the Railroad Woods, and were commanded by Lieutenant Stewart himself. Just south of these and across the pike from the stone house were the two three-inch rifles of Lieutenant Benjamin W. Wilber's section of Battery L, 1st New York Light Artillery. South of these guns were the six Napoleons of Captain Greenlief T. Stevens' Fifth Maine Battery, and three three-inch rifles of Captain James Cooper's Battery B, 1st Pennsylvania Light Artillery. Also, south of the Seminary were the four other guns of Battery L, 1st New York Light Artillery, under the command of Lieutenant George Breck. All in all, 21 artillery pieces were lined up from just south of the Seminary buildings to a point just north of the railroad cut. "These guns were brimmed with shell or double shotted with canister; every man was at his station, and they were awaiting this very opportunity."[7]

Mixed in with the guns and spread out across an orchard near the pike were the three Pennsylvania regiments of the "Bucktail Brigade" (143th, 149th, and 150th Pennsylvania) now under the command of Colonel Edmund Dana, and the remnants of the famous "Iron Brigade" (19th Indiana, 24th Michigan, 2nd, 6th and 7th Wisconsin). These units had just moments before been driven off McPherson Ridge and were now trying to rally around the artillery along the ridge. Colonel

Dana ordered ammunition handed out, and every man was resupplied with "60 rounds."[8]

The 143rd Pennsylvania made its stand with the guns of Lieutenant Davison, near the "Peach Orchard," and directly in front of the Thompson House. Private Frank Foster of Co. H recalled that at "about 3:45 [p.m.] the boys" formed in "back of a four board fence at the old stone house."[9] The regiment was under the command of 37 year old Lieutenant Colonel John Musser. In a letter to a friend written shortly after the battle, he described the situation.

> It was near a house on the Chambersburg Road, we had to cross the road in front, and endure heavy cannonading from a Rebel battery with no small peppering of minies and canister, but the resolve, was in the heart of every man, to stand by and save the battery [Stewart's Battery B] from the advancing Rebels, who were now seen coming in force on the right of the road, briskly loading and firing as they came. The [Rebel] battery was thundering shell and shot among us, some bursting over our heads, others among the trees cutting them off, then as if not satisfied, bursting and scattering the pieces in every direction, killing and wounding as they went. Others came plowing through under our feet lifting men up in the air to find when they came down their graves already open. Still the 143rd stood up to the work in hand....[10]

Across the railroad cut, and just a little northwest of these pieces were the other three guns of Battery B under the command of Lieutenant James Stewart. He watched as the Southerners approached in "fine style." All along the line, the blue clad soldiers "did not fire a musket until they came within a distance of about four hundred yards." Lieutenant Stewart noted that Davison "withheld his fire until the enemy had reached what we thought about three hundred yards, when he opened fire."[11] A soldier in the 2nd Wisconsin remembered the scene:

> Almost at the same moment, as if every lanyard was pulled by the same hand, this line of artillery opened, and Seminary Ridge blazed with a solid sheet of flame, and the missiles of death that swept its western slopes no human beings could endure. After a few moments of the belching of the artillery, the blinding smoke shut out the sun and obstructed the view. We of the infantry fell into line between the artillery sections and assisted with our musketry, keeping up the fire until our pieces grew hot in our hands, and the darkness, as of night, had settled upon us.[12]

As the enemy lines got closer, "the musketry burst from Seminary Ridge; every shot was fired with care, and Stewart's men with the regularity of a machine, worked their guns upon the enemy." Davison ordered his guns to move forward toward the pike and take up a position that would enfilade the entire Southern line. Colonel Dawes of the 6th Wisconsin, whose regiment was in support of Battery B, described that the oncoming Rebels "came half way down this slope, wavered, began to fire, then to scatter and then to run, and how our men did yell, 'come on Johnny, come on.'"[13]

Battery B, 4th United States Artillery, was made up mostly of volunteer soldiers from the regiments of the Iron Brigade, and not from the regular army as the name might imply. Nonetheless, by the time of the Gettysburg Campaign these men were veterans of many a hard fought battle, and were considered to be one of the best artillery units in the army. During the late 1880s the *National Tribune*, a veterans' newspaper printed in Washington D.C., ran a series of articles entitled "The Story of a Cannoneer" telling of the exploits of Battery B.[14] The author, Augustus Buell, claimed to be a member of the battery, and for years this work has been used by historians as a first hand account of the desperate fighting along Seminary Ridge.[15] However, there is overwhelming evidence to indicate that Buell was never in Battery B, and was not even present at the Battle of Gettysburg. His account, accurate as it might be, must have been put together by interviewing surviving members of the battery, and by using other first hand accounts of the fighting. He may have included himself to give the story more of a personal touch, or he may have been purposefully trying to deceive the public.[16] Whatever the motives, his account of the fighting is probably one of the most exciting accounts of an artilleryman in battle during the Civil War.

> We were formed in a small field just west of Mrs. Thompson's dooryard, and our guns raked the road to the top of the low crest....At this moment Davison, bleeding from two desperate wounds, and so weak that one of the men had to hold him up on his feet (one ankle being totally shattered by a bullet), ordered us to form the half battery, action left, by wheeling on the left gun as a pivot, so as to bring the half battery on a line with the Cashtown Pike, muzzles facing

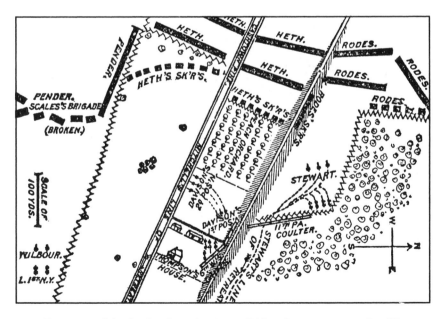

Diagram of the battle along Seminary Ridge, from Augustus Buell's **The Cannoneer (1890).**

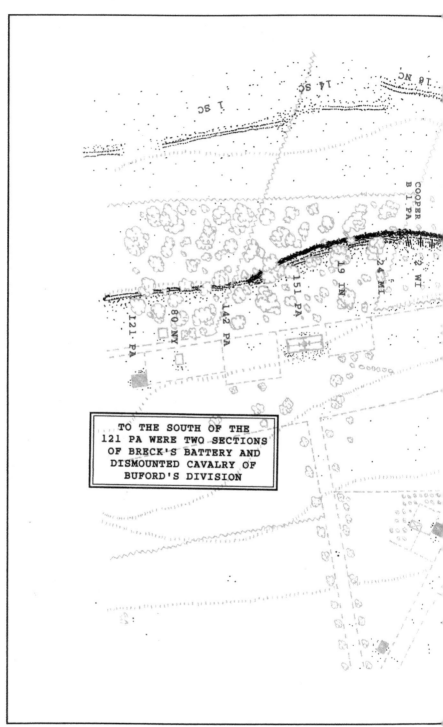

TO THE SOUTH OF THE
121 PA WERE TWO SECTIONS
OF BRECK'S BATTERY AND
DISMOUNTED CAVALRY OF
BUFORD'S DIVISION

The defense of Seminary Ridge, 4:00 pm, July 1, 1863.

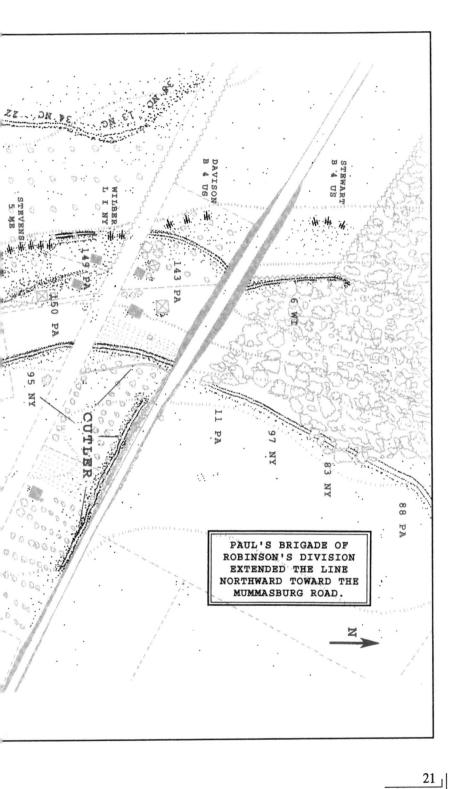

PAUL'S BRIGADE OF
ROBINSON'S DIVISION
EXTENDED THE LINE
NORTHWARD TOWARD THE
MUMMASBURG ROAD.

south, his object being to rake the front of the Rebel line closing in on us from that side....

...[T]his change of front gave us a clean rake along the Rebel line for a whole brigade length, but it exposed us to the raking volleys of their infantry near the pike, who at that moment began to get up again and come on. Then for seven or eight minutes ensued probably the most desperate fight ever waged between artillery and infantry at close range without a particle of cover on either side. They gave us volley after volley in front and flank, and we gave them double canister as fast as we could load. The 6th Wisconsin and the 11th Pennsylvania men crawled up on the bank of the cut or behind the rail fence in rear of Stewart's caissons and joined their musketry to our canister, while from the north side of the cut flashed the chain-lightning of the Old Man's [Stewart] half-battery in one solid streak!

...[T]he dauntless Davison [was] on foot among the guns, cheering the men, praising this one and that one, and ever and anon profanely exhorting us to "feed it to 'em, God Damn 'em; feed it to 'em!" The very guns became things of life— not implements, but comrades. Every man was doing the work of two or three....

Up and down the line men reeling and falling; splinters flying from wheels and axles where bullets hit; in rear, horses tearing and plunging, mad with wounds or terror; drivers yelling, shells bursting, shot shrieking overhead, howling about our ears or throwing up great clouds of dust where they struck; the musketry crashing on three sides of us; bullets hissing, humming and whistling everywhere; cannon roaring; all crash on crash and peal on peal, smoke, dust splinters, blood, wreck and carnage indescribable; but the brass guns of Old B still bellowed and not a man or boy flinched or faltered! Every man's shirt soaked with sweat and many of them sopped with blood from wounds not severe enough to make such bulldogs "let go"—bareheaded, sleeves rolled up, faces blackened-oh! If such a picture could be spread on canvas to the life! Out in front of us an undulating field, filled almost as far as the eye could reach with a long, low gray line creeping toward us, fairly fringed with flame!

On every side the passion, rage and frenzy of fearless men or reckless boys devoted to slaughter or doomed to death! The same sun that a day before had been shining to cure the wheat-sheves of the harvest of peace, now glared to pierce the gray pall of battle's powder smoke or to bloat the corpses of battle's victims. How strange it is to think of now![17]

At the time of its publication "The Story of a Cannoneer" was widely acclaimed as an "accurate and factual" account of the fighting. In fact, James Stewart, the commander of the battery itself, wrote a letter to the *National Tribune* praising the articles for their content.[18] It is of course not known if he realized at the time that Buell was a ghostwriter, or if in fact, Stewart was one of the men Buell had interviewed. In any case, today, it remains one of the most colorful accounts ever written of the fighting around the Thompson House on July 1, 1863.

As for the Southern soldiers who felt the brunt of this carnage, they were the five regiments of Alfred M. Scales' North Carolina brigade (13th, 16th, 22nd, 34th, and 38th North Carolina). The left of this brigade rested on the Chambersburg Pike,

Sketch from **The Cannoneer** *(1890). The view is looking southeast, (note the Thompson House in the left background) and depicts Lieutenant James Davison with his three guns along the Chambersburg Pike. The original caption reads "Feed it to 'em, Boys!"*

and as it moved across the valley toward Seminary Ridge General Scales recalled it was suddenly hit by a fire that was "terribly destructive" to his men.[19]

> ...[We] commenced the descent just opposite the Theological Seminary. Here the brigade encountered a most terrific fire of grape and shell on our flank, and grape and musketry in our front. Every discharge made sad havoc in our lines, but still we pressed on at a double-quick until we reached the bottom, a distance of about 75 yards from the ridge we had just crossed, and about the same distance from the college, in our front. Here I received a painful wound from a piece of shell, and was disabled. Our line was broken up, and now only a squad here and there marked the place where regiments had rested. Every field officer of the brigade save one had been disabled, and the...list of casualties will attest sufficiently the terrible ordeal through which the brigade passed....[20]

With the wounding of General Scales, command fell to Colonel William Lowrance of the 34th North Carolina, who found that the brigade numbered only about 500 men, and very few officers. "Many companies were without a single officer to lead them or to inquire after them." Colonel Lowrance complained that "in this depressed, dilapidated, and almost unorganized condition I took command."[21]

The 13th North Carolina was severely cut up in the slaughter. Adjutant Nathan S. Smith recalled that when the regiment got to within "75 yards of the enemy" the "...men were ordered to lie down. Of the one hundred and eighty men in the regiment, one hundred and fifty were killed and wounded, leaving only thirty men..." commanded by just two officers.[22] Lieutenant Thomas D. Lattimore of Company F, 34th North Carolina recalled that his regiment was "exposed to a deadly enfilading fire from artillery on the left and infantry in front, from behind breastworks." Because of this "thunderous fire...for the first time in its history, the brigade was repulsed."[23]

While Stewart's Battery was ripping away at the flank of Scales' Brigade, others were pouring a deadly fire in from the front. Lieutenant James Gardner of Cooper's Battery remembered that "in descending the slope," the Rebels "encountered a most terribly destructive and withering fire from our guns...by which Scales was halted with heavy loss, his brigade thrown into confusion and broken up."[24] Corporal Robert K. Beecham of the 2nd Wisconsin was more descriptive in his account remarking that "the charging Confederates were brave men,—in fact, no braver ever faced death in any cause and none ever faced more certain death!"[25]

> Not a Confederate reached our line. After we had ceased firing and the smoke of battle had lifted, we looked again, but the charging Confederates were not there. Only the dead and dying remained on the bloody slopes of Seminary Ridge.[26]

Monument to Stewart's Battery B, 4th U.S. Artillery, situated just west of General Lee's Headquarters Museum.

PART IV

Retreat

Although the center of the Union line had held, things were not going so well for the Northern soldiers fighting on its flanks. Corporal Beecham of the 2nd Wisconsin recalled that "for a few brief moments above Seminary Ridge...we hailed that dear old flag...as a harbinger of victory and peace." But "the smoke of battle still enshrouded" the field and it was hard for these soldiers to see what was going on a few hundred feet away.[1] Suddenly, someone shouted:

> "Look there! What troops are those?" pointing away to the northeast. We all looked, of course, and we saw the whole valley north of the city, from Seminary Ridge on the west to Rock Creek on the east, alive with rapidly advancing troops, bearing triumphantly above them the saucy battle-flags of the Confederacy...still nearer, in the outskirts of the city we caught a glimpse of the Stars and Stripes disappearing behind the walls and buildings, borne on by our troops, retiring in haste and confusion.[2]

The retreating troops referred to by Beecham were those of the Union Eleventh Corps. Unknown to these soldiers at the time, was that fact that they also would be forced to retreat. Simultaneous attacks by units of Pender's and Rodes' Confederate divisions had just crumbled the flanks of the Union First Corps. While the "murderous fire" from the batteries on Seminary Ridge had brought Scales' North Carolinians to a complete stop, it had only slowed down the South Carolina brigade of Colonel Abner Perrin.[3] As these troops (1st, 12th, 13th, 14th South Carolina) moved across the valley in front of the Seminary, Colonel Perrin recalled that "the brigade received the most destructive fire of musketry I have ever been exposed to."[4] James Fitz James Caldwell of the 1st South Carolina said later that the artillery "opened on us with a fatal accuracy" but "still we advanced" as "shell and canister continued to rain upon us."[5]

The left of this brigade was hit especially hard. The 14th South Carolina, the closest regiment to Scales' men, was "staggered for a moment by the severity and destructiveness of the enemy's musketry." It looked to Colonel Perrin "as though this regiment was entirely destroyed."[6] After the war the lieutenant colonel of the 14th South Carolina, Joseph Newton Brown wrote of this experience.

> ...[T]he line of breastworks in front became a sheet of fire and smoke, sending its leaden missiles of death in the faces of men who had often, but never so terribly met it before. The impenetrable masses of artillery and infantry in front and on the flank of General Scales impeded his progress, enfilading and

sweeping his whole front....In like manner, on our right, General Lane was held in check, and the cavalry on his flank threatened certain destruction if his advance continued...the want of support on the right and left...exposed [us] to a raking enfilade fire from both right and left without abatement in front. To stop was destruction. To retreat was disaster. To go forward was "orders."[7]

At this critical moment, Colonel Abner Perrin "spurred" his horse through the brigade, "and with his sword flashing in the evening sunshine," personally led the 1st South Carolina in a charge. He directed Major Comillus W. McCreary in command of the 1st, to "oblique to the right," thereby avoiding the rail barricade in front of the Seminary, break through the thin defense on the other side, and enfilade the Union line. Colonel Perrin was most pleased with this movement and remarked that it "was done most effectually...the enemy here was completely routed."[8]

While the 1st South Carolina was outflanking the barricade, the 14th was assailing directly upon it. "The dead, the wounded, the dying were falling at every step." Because the Union breastworks were in the shape of a semi-circle, the lines were "curved slightly back on either side near to the crest of the Ridge, and this made the Seminary the salient or point of attack...here the brigade threw itself against it with all its fury. Here the opposing forces grappled with each other, one determined to hold its position, and the other determined to take it."[9]

One of the Northern regiments positioned in the rail entrenchment directly in front of Colonel Brown's men was the 151st Pennsylvania. During the dedication of their monument, Lieutenant Colonel George F. McFarland described the scene as his men desperately tried to hold their position.

...[T]he enemy extended far to our left and soon made it impossible for us to remain longer in our enfiladed position, and I ordered our regiment back in time to escape the flank fire. My horse had been shot under me, but I still remained unhurt. I accompanied my regiment back to within a rod or two of the north end of the Seminary, then stopped, and stooping down to reconnoiter the enemy before passing beyond the building, thus facing the front, I received the volley from the left flank, from which I had saved the regiment by ordering it back. This fire knocked both legs from under me, badly shattering both....[10]

The "shattered remnant" of the 151st Pennsylvania, along with the other regiments that were being forced from their position along Seminary Ridge, started their retreat toward the town.[11] Now, as one Confederate soldier so aptly put it, "the Rebel turn came to kill."[12] With the breakthrough at the Seminary "thousands of hostile bayonets made their appearance around the sides of the buildings." The entire Union line was now beginning to crumble, and without reserves to plug the gaps there was little General Doubleday could do but order his troops to retire through the town and regroup on Cemetery Hill.[13]

Unfortunately for the retreating troops of the First Corps, very few had even heard of Cemetery Hill, and most had no idea how to get there. When these troops had been rushed onto the battlefield earlier that day, they had skirted the town to the south and west, and no unit of the First Corps had actually passed through Gettysburg. Now with the fall of the Seminary defenses, the avenue which had

Ca. 1870 engraving by A.R. Waud, illustrating the 14th South Carolina's encounter with the 151st Pennsylvania at the breastworks in front of the Lutheran Theological Seminary. From an original engraving in a John B. Bachelder scrapbook owned by the Author.

brought these men onto the field was closed. To the Northern soldiers, who, for the first time in their lives were entering the town, Gettysburg must have looked like a maze. The chaos that ensued is today virtually ignored by historians, but for this study it is critical. The position around the Thompson House and the railroad cut would be the last held by Union troops on the first day's field.

For Colonel Wainwright, now came the huge task of getting the artillery off the ridge and through the town. Wainwright recalled that it was a "wonder" that any got off at all.[14] There were many close calls and one three-inch rifle from Wilber's section of Battery L, 1st New York Light Artillery, was actually overrun and captured by troops of Perrin's South Carolina Brigade, very near Mrs. Thompson's house. Ironically, the gun's serial number was #1, the first three-inch rifle accepted into service by the Ordnance Department.[15]

With all the confusion and the smoke of battle, the troops located near the Thompson House were not informed of the retreat until things were very critical. Colonel Dawes of the 6th Wisconsin, whose unit was just behind Stewart's Battery B, remembered that when the order to retreat came he was "astonished."

> The cheers of defiance along the line of the first corps, on Seminary Ridge, had scarcely died away. But a glance over the field to our right and rear was sufficient. There the troops of the eleventh corps appeared in full retreat, and long lines of Confederates, with fluttering banners and shining steel, were

sweeping forward in pursuit of them without let or hindrance. It was a close race which could reach Gettysburg first, ourselves, or the rebel troops of Ewell's corps, who pursued our eleventh corps.[16]

The situation was now much worse than even Colonel Dawes realized. Not only was the Eleventh Corps in full retreat, the right of the First Corps at Oak Ridge, had just been driven in by a brigade of North Carolinians (2nd, 4th, 14th, and 30th North Carolina) under the command of Brigadier General Stephen Dodson Ramseur. The Seminary had fallen to Pender's Division, and now there was a new threat from the west. Brigadier General Junius Daniel's Brigade (32nd, 43rd, 45th, 53rd North Carolina, and 2nd NC Battalion), who had earlier been engaged against the Union troops holding the McPherson farm, was now approaching the railroad cut from the west. The position around the Thompson House was being attacked from three sides and things were beginning to get pretty hot. Lieutenant Colonel John Musser of the 143rd Pennsylvania described the scene.

> By this time the enemy had advanced on our right, to within fifty yards of one of our batteries stationed there, and the cry was "save our battery...." We turned upon them like tigers regardless of danger, with a determination in the mind of every man, to save the battery or die in the effort, and our effort was crowned with success, some pulled the guns away, while others kept the enemy back. There was a perfect shower of shells, shot and musketry poured into us, from all sides cutting the hay down around us, bursting over our heads and plowing the earth up beneath us....[17]

The 6th Wisconsin was positioned in the Railroad Woods, just north of the cut and very near the 143rd. Much of what was happening on other parts of the battlefield was hidden from their view. However, as Colonel Dawes faced "the regiment to the rear" and left the protection of the woods on the eastern slopes of Seminary Ridge, he became painfully aware of how desperate the situation actually was.

> ...I marched in line of battle over the open fields toward the town. We were north of the railroad, and our direction separated us from other regiments of our corps. If we had desired to attack Ewell's twenty thousand men with our two hundred, we could not have moved more directly toward them. We knew nothing about a Cemetery Hill. We could see only that the on-coming lines of the enemy were encircling us in a horseshoe.[18]

As the infantry began to pull away, Lieutenant Stewart hurriedly limbered his guns and moved them over the ridge to a position where he hoped to cross the railroad embankment, but problems soon developed.

> I moved [my guns] down through the timber, running a short distance parallel with the railroad cut, and then attempted to cross. I did not know at the time that the cut was full of large rocks. However, the men got the first two pieces over, but in getting over the third, the pintle hook broke and the trail fell to the ground. As this happened a party of rebels came running out of the timber adjoining, shouting: "halt that piece!" We were all completely surprised, but

one of the men was fully equal to the occasion, and shouted back: "Don't you see that the piece is halted?" I had the leading pieces brought back up on the road and opened upon them, when they took to cover very quickly. In the meantime, the men were taking the prolonge off the trail and tying up the gun to the limber.

When the pintle hook broke, I felt that we would never be able to get the gun out of the cut, as it took us a long time to disengage the prolonge from the trail; then we had to get the limber out of the cut, then the gun; then we had to tie the trail to the rear of the limber; and during all this time the enemy were firing upon us at not more than one hundred yards; and just as we got the gun out of the cut, the enemy made a dash, this time getting within fifty or sixty yards, killing one driver (the driver of the swing team), and seriously wounding the wheel driver and two horses, which again caused delay. But the two pieces kept firing at them all the time, and I will say right here that if ever men stayed by their guns, it certainly was then.[19]

Luckily for Stewart, many retreating infantrymen saw the trouble he was in and came to his aid. Lieutenant George Grant of the 88th Pennsylvania recalled that they "made a determined stand to save Stewart's Battery, which had lingered too long and was in danger of being captured."[20] With the help of these infantrymen Battery B was finally able to get their gun out of the cut and start down the Chambersburg Pike into town. The smoke of battle clouded the field, and it was impossible to tell friend from foe until at close range. In all this confusion Lieutenant Stewart became concerned about the whereabouts of Davison and his other three guns.

After we got well on the road, I told the sergeant to move to town and I would go back and see what Davison was doing, as I could not believe he would have left without informing me of the fact. I started in the direction of the Thompson House, but on getting pretty near there, I saw the place was occupied by the enemy. On seeing me, they shouted, "surrender!" But as I had not gone there for that purpose, I wheeled my horse and started him off as fast as he could go. It was my intention to catch up with my sergeant, but I found that I could not reach the road as it was occupied by the enemy—in fact, the enemy was closing in on all sides.

Lieutenant James Stewart, commander of Battery B, 4th U.S. Artillery. **From The Cannoneer (1890).**

On seeing that I could not make my way to where my half battery had gone, I started across the field, when the first thing I observed in front of me was a high fence, and as I could not go either to the right or left without being made a prisoner, I headed my horse for it, and he took the leap in splendid style. As he was making the jump I was struck on the thigh with a piece of shell. The shock was terrible, and I thought at first my leg was broken....[21]

While Lieutenant Stewart did narrowly escape, many others were not so lucky that day. Colonel John Musser, in command of the 143rd Pennsylvania, also wrote of this hectic retreat from the ridge west of town.

> A few minutes more and we would have been surrounded, they were on both sides of us and as near the town as we were. A high artificial road lay across a wide meadow between the Peach Orchard and the town. It broke the enfilading fire on our right, we took the left side, and moved rapidly to town but in good order. There was no use in fighting any longer. The enemy had deployed and we were trapped. The town was before us, the enemy on either side, and behind us.[22]

That "high artificial road" was the unfinished railroad embankment that led from Seminary Ridge into town. The Southern soldiers could also see the noose that was beginning to close around the Federals. "We had the Yankees like partridges in a nest, and the only way they could get out was up the railroad" recalled a man in Ramseur's Brigade.[23] General Ramseur quickly realized the opportunity he was presented with and ordered up a battery of artillery. "In a few minutes it was throwing shell at the railroad," where the thousands of Union soldiers who were retreating towards town made a glaring target.[24]

Perrin's South Carolinians, who were now east of the Seminary buildings were laying down such a heavy fire that it simply swept the Chambersburg Pike of Union infantry. Colonel Wainwright remembered that this fire forced the Northern troops over the railroad embankment and onto the other side where they thought it safer.[25] But when these men reached the north side of the railroad they were hit by the infantry sweeping down on that side as well. A heavy artillery fire was now beginning to fall into the retreating Northern masses. One Confederate colonel thought that he could "almost hear their bones crunch under the shot and shell" of the Southern batteries.[26] "It was here" remembered Colonel William Robinson of the 7th Wisconsin, that "I met with the heaviest losses from the regiment during the day."[27] Charles Fuller of Co. E said that "there was scarcely a man but what had his clothes struck somewhere...it seemed almost a miracle how any of us escaped."[28] Captain Henry Young of Co. F remembered that during this retreat things were so chaotic "it was impossible for several days to tell who was killed and who was taken prisoner...for men were falling thick and fast around us and there was no time to pick them up or look to see who they were."[29]

As bad as things were for the troops of the First Corps they were about to get worse. Brigadier General George Doles and his Georgians were joining the fight. This brigade (4th, 12th, 21st, and 44th Georgia), part of Rodes' Division, had been detached, helping Early's Division rout the Eleventh Corps. Now with the situation well in hand, and Early's men continuing the pursuit of the troops north of town, Doles was returning to help the rest of his division. As his men moved toward the "theological college" across the open fields directly northwest of town, Doles could plainly see Northern soldiers withdrawing their "forces from the college hill to the railroad." He moved his brigade "rapidly by the left flank, to cut him off from the town."[30] If a junction had been created by the troops of Doles' Brigades from the north and Perrin's Brigade from the south, the entire First Corps may have been captured. As it was these converging forces created a gauntlet that none of the retreating Northern soldiers would ever forget.

The men of the Second Division, First Corps, under the command of General John Cleveland Robinson had the farthest distance of any Union troops to cross on their retreat. Their position had been north of the railroad cut extending across Oak Ridge to the Mummasburg Road. When these battle weary veterans were driven off the field by overwhelming Confederate forces, they retired in the direction they had come. Lieutenant George W. Grant, of the 88th Pennsylvania was one of these men, and years later wrote of an experience that was shared by a great many of his comrades that day.

"Not knowing that the left wing had been pressed back, a number of us started in the direction of the Seminary, from which point we entered the fight, but the Rebel line had swept over the ridge; the avenue of escape was cut off, and we were made prisoners of war."[31]

For many, this fatal mistake allowed the victorious troops of Rodes and Pender to cut off their last route of retreat. Only upon arriving at the railroad cut did many of the Northern soldiers realize their predicament. Lieutenant Wilbur Judd of the 97th New York recalled the "sad disaster" that occurred next:

> ...[T]he order was given to fall back to the railroad....We found that they had turned our left, also, and our only escape was to follow the railroad into town. Our regiment was the last to leave and the last into town. Col. Spofford, Capt. Eggleston and myself were at the rear of the column, and when we were out of the wood on the railroad, the rebels were twenty rods nearer the town than we were. The Colonel and Captain did not think best to run the gauntlet and turned the opposite way into a deep cut for protection; but I did not fancy the idea of being taken and went into town; but I beg leave to state that it was running the gauntlet in the strict sense of the word. The bullets were flying from each side in a perfect shower. The air seemed so filled that it seemed almost impossible to breathe without inhaling them. Some one fell beside me almost every step.[32]

Lieutenant Judd was not the only soldier who would remember the "gauntlet." Account after account uses that one word to describe the hopeless situation the First Corps found itself in. Private Austin Stearns of the 13th Massachusetts also wrote of "running the gauntlet." "I started back. The field was filled with wounded men and those who were not, all trying to escape the anaconda that had almost entwined us in its folds."[33] Unfortunately for the First Corps, it was impossible for everyone

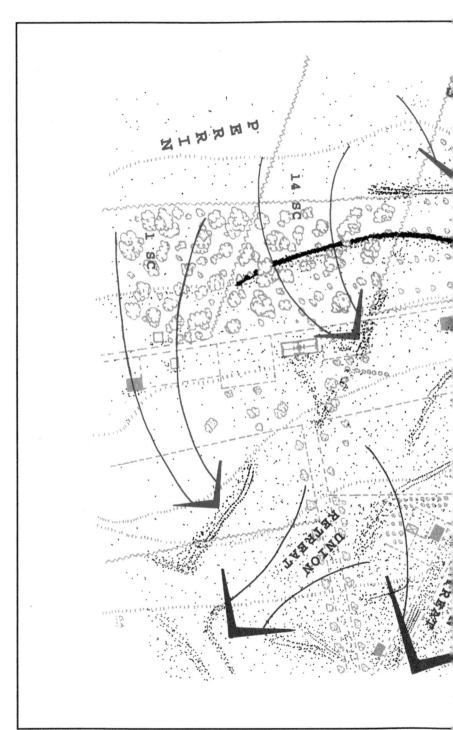

The Gauntlet: Retreat of the 1st Corps, 4:30 pm, July 1, 1863.

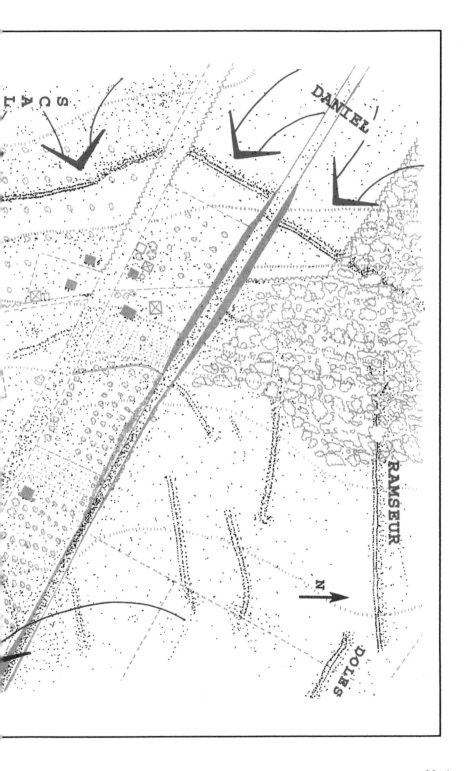

to get away. Many Union soldiers were still in and around the railroad cut when the Rebels encircled it. The 16th Maine Regiment, who were placed as a rear guard to General John Robinson's Division were one of the last organized Northern units to leave Seminary Ridge. The adjutant of the 16th Maine thought they were "sacrificed to steady the retreat."

> ...[I]t was only a matter of minutes before the gray lines threatened to crush us....We got to the railroad cut, which offered a means of defense against the Rebels following us, but just then we saw gray troops making in from the west, and they saw us. We were caught between two fires. It was the end.[34]

Closing together, the Southern battlelines struck the Union soldiers in the cut simultaneously. "Ewell's men appeared upon the north side of the cut and Hill's upon the south so nearly at the same time that both lines, with leveled muskets, claimed the prisoners." The colonel of the 16th Maine was summoned upon to surrender by a "tall skirmisher from Alabama" who shouted "throw down that sword or I will blow your brains out."[35]

> Summoned to surrender, Colonel [Charles] Tilden plunged his sword into the ground and broke it short off at the hilt, and directed the destruction of the colors. A Rebel officer sprang to seize the flag, when the men, once more for the last time, closed around the priceless emblems, and in a moment of fury, rent the staves in twain and threw the pieces at the officer's feet. Eager hands from every direction seized the banners and tore them piece by piece beyond reclaim or recognition.[36]

"From the position we occupied when we were surrounded we could not see how a single man got away" noted Lieutenant Lewis Bisbee. Colonel Tilden made the remark that on that day "every man who did his duty was either killed, wounded, or captured."[37] The capture of Union troops in the railroad cut is also mentioned in several Confederate reports written within days of the battle. Captain James A. Hopkins of the 45th North Carolina described an incident which is undoubtedly the capture of the 16th Maine.

> ...[Our regiment] was next moved so as to obtain a position perpendicular to the railroad cut, and made a charge on the wood in our front, capturing 188 prisoners in this place and several smaller squads in other places. The flag of the Twentieth North Carolina Regiment was recaptured by Capt. A[lexander] H. Gallaway, and handed by him to a member of that regiment. We also captured a very fine flag-staff and tassels; the remnants of what had been a fine Yankee flag were lying in different places.[38]

Officially the 16th Maine had 164 men captured at the battle, most of these at the cut.[39] But the 16th Maine was not alone, and the true number of prisoners surrounded in that area was much higher. According to Lieutenant Colonel William Gaston Lewis of the 43rd North Carolina "at the railroad cut 400 or 500 prisoners surrendered to the brigade."[40] Every regiment in the First Corps had a considerable amount of men taken prisoner on the first day of the battle. Of its 28 infantry regiments engaged, 24 had fifty or more men captured. The First Brigade of the

Detail of ca. 1890 photo taken from Glatfelter Hall on the Gettysburg College campus looking toward the Thompson House on Seminary Ridge. The stone house can be seen between the house and barn of Henry Dustman. Note the Railroad embankment in the foreground. **ACHS.**

Post war view looking west toward the Seminary Ridge Railroad Cut. The site of the largest mass capture of Northern soldiers during the battle. **ACHS.**

Second Division, commanded by Brigadier General Gabriel R. Paul, suffered the highest percentage loss of any brigade, Union or Confederate, during the entire battle. Retreating back across Seminary Ridge and through the town this brigade had 40% of its men captured. Colonel Gilbert Prey of the 104th New York, among those who did escape, said he made it only by the skin of his teeth, running the gauntlet through a storm of shot and shell.[41] As the victorious Southerners pushed through the town many more straggling Union soldiers were picked up, as they tried to find protection in buildings or alleys. In all, over 2,000 men of the First Corps were captured at the battle. Although many historians choose to ignore that fact, it is much greater than the loss of the Eleventh Corps. However, these figures do not include the number of men who were lying wounded on the field, or in the temporary field hospitals, that were captured when the Confederates overran the town. The true number of captured on the First Day of the Battle of Gettysburg by Lee's army may be as high as 5,000 men.[42] Certainly it ranks as one of the most productive days in the history of the Army of Northern Virginia.

Post war view of the Chambersburg Pike looking west. This area was known as "the Gauntlet" in many contemporary accounts. ACHS.

PART V

Robert E. Lee

As the battle passed through town and onto the ridges south of it, the sounds of musketry and artillery on Seminary Ridge were replaced by the moans and screams of the wounded and dying. Many of the accounts written by retreating Northern soldiers describe the feeling of leaving their wounded comrades behind. A drummer boy in the 150th Pennsylvania wrote afterwards that as he retreated "along the cut...[the] dead were scattered around on all sides; and the wounded [were] crying piteously for help."[1] John Musser of the 143rd Pennsylvania wrote that "it had cost many a brave boy his life, and others were left wounded and bleeding to the tender mercy of the then victorious enemy. We had no time to take care of them. We could give only a parting glance of sympathy."[2] Lieutenant Stewart of Battery B remarked that "then for the first time that day did I realize what the horrors of war meant....I could not bring my wounded with me, and the beseeching looks that these men gave me quite unnerved me, and I was sorry indeed to leave them to their fate."[3]

The fields around the Thompson House were littered with wounded. Every structure in the vicinity was immediately converted into a hospital merely by the fact that wounded men crawled into them in great quantities. Casper Henry Dustman, whose house was just east of the Thompson residence on Seminary Ridge, told many stories of his experiences during the battle. "His house—a brick one—was used as a hospital on the first day," and his barn had "several holes in it, made by shot and shell."[4] In later years he wrote of a strange incident that occurred to him during "the afternoon of July 1st, 1863."

> ...a soldier came to me and said, "there is an old man laying over there on the cellar door, (pointing across the road to the little brick house), who wants to see you." "Who in the world wants to see me now, in all this fighting!" However, I lost no time and went over. There lay John Burns on the cellar door. I said to him "why John, what is the matter." He said, "oh Henry I took my gun and went out to fight the rebels, and got wounded." At the same time, showing me his ankle. Doubting his story, I asked where his gun was. He said, "I took my pocket knife and buried it near that sour apple tree," at the same time showing me where he was wounded. "I then crept from there on my hands and knees to this cellar door. Go and tell my wife to get a wagon to take me home in." I said, "that will be something to do." However, I went.[5]

Detail of photo on page 36 showing the Sheads House, the Dustman House and the Dustman Barn. ACHS.

Although Dustman could not convince Mrs. Burns to come out and get John, he was later able to stop a wagon traveling down the pike and have him taken to his home. Sixty-nine-year-old John Burns, a civilian of the town of Gettysburg, had been wounded three times while fighting in defense of his country with members of the Union First Corps along McPherson Ridge. Burns would later recall that the Dustman House was "full of wounded rebels."[6]

The Lutheran Theological Seminary was turned into a large field hospital, and would remain so for several months after the battle. The professors' houses at either end of the Seminary complex were also used, and James Thompson's house was so "filled with wounded and dying men of the 1st Corps" that his wife and two children, the youngest just one day old at the time of the battle, were forced to flee their home.[7] Samuel and Hannah Foulk, who lived a short distance from Mary, also had a house "filled with wounded men on the first day" of the battle. The children were sent to the basement while the parents tried to care for the wounded. The fences on their property and from all the property around were broken up and used for firewood or breastworks.[8] Across the road from the Foulk residence was that of Elias Sheads. His daughter, Carrie, had been using part of the house as a school for girls, but with the coming of battle it was converted to a hospital, and in all, over 70 injured soldiers were cared for in the structure.[9] And of course with her close proximity to the heaviest fighting, wounded from both sides were taken to Mrs. Thompson's house. In an account written at the turn of the century, Catherine Foster described the active role played by Mary in taking care of the wounded.

> Old Lady Thompson, occupant of Lee's Headquarters, however, never deserted her house. Her house and lot were filled with wounded and dying during the first day; she remained to care for them, and had a daughter [Hannah] living at the foot of the hill, who baked up a barrel of flour into bread, which she carried up the hill to the wounded, and refused to cease doing so during the three

days...until her clothes were perforated with bullets and yet she would not be dissuaded, said, "In God is my trust." All her clothes and bedding except those on her person were used in dressing the wounded and her carpets in wrapping the dead for burial. An empty stone house and fenceless yard were all that was left the widow of seventy years.[10]

It is interesting to note that in a claim made to the government after the war for losses to her property, besides damage done to her yard and garden, Mrs. Thompson also made a claim for pillow cases, bolsters, sheets, blankets, cotton rags, wearing apparel, and 18 yards of cotton carpet, which would seem to suggest that she was in fact taking care of the wounded.[11]

Ca. 1880 photo of Sarah Elizabeth Foulk (1861-1910). The youngest of the five Foulk children, she and her family "kept in [the] Cellar" while the battle raged around their house on the afternoon of July 1st. **Courtesy of Evelyn D. Hughes.**

Woodcut made from a M.B. Brady photo taken shortly after the battle. The view is looking east from a position near the Dustman House. Note the Sheads and Foulk Houses in the foreground. **Author's collection.**

Of course today, when we think of the Thompson House, we think of it as the headquarters of Confederate Commander General Robert E. Lee. By the time he made his appearance on Seminary Ridge on July 1, 1863, his army had been successful in routing the Union forces from the fields west and north of the town, had captured Gettysburg itself, and were threatening to attack the reforming Union position along Cemetery Ridge. James Power Smith, a Confederate staff officer described Lee in detail as he arrived on the battlefield that afternoon.

> ...he sat on his well-bred iron gray, Traveler, and looked across the fields eastward....A rod or two away, I sat in my saddle and caught the picture which has not faded from memory, and grows more distinct as the years go by. He was fifty-six years old, with a superb physique, five feet and eleven and one-half inches in height, about one hundred and seventy-five pounds in weight, and in perfect health....He was a gentleman by blood and breeding, so truly that he was unmindful of it. He was plain and neat in his uniform of gray, so careful of his dress that there was nothing to attract attention. He wore a hat of gray felt, with medium brim and his boots fitted neatly, coming to his knee with a border of fair leather an inch wide....He was a kingly man whom all men who came into his presence expected to obey.[12]

With the arrival of Lee, the Thompson House would again be thrown onto center stage. Due to its location on Seminary Ridge, and alongside the Chambersburg Pike, "the main western artery leading into town," it made a perfect site for the commanding general to establish his headquarters. As one historian has pointed out "a better location for directing the battle could not have been selected."[13] Sergeant Martin V. Gander of Co. C 39th Battalion Virginia Cavalry, who was acting as a courier and scout for Lee's staff, recalled that he "placed four guards around the old stone house on the hill, the personal headquarters of Gen. Lee the evening of July 1, 1863 about 5.30 pm. at the command of Adj. Gen. Taylor, who was in the field headquarters across the street."[14] Colonel Charles Marshall, an aide-de-camp for Lee, also remembered that "General Lee slept that night [July 1st] in a small stone house east of the Seminary Ridge and just north of the Chambersburg Pike, his staff bivouacking in an orchard near by."[15] About a "half dozen small tents" were set up by members of his staff "a little way from the roadside" and in close proximity to the Thompson House.[16] Undoubtedly one of these tents was that of General Robert E. Lee, and there are accounts to indicate that during the battle he did spend time in his tent, and the tents of his staff. But there are also accounts that he used the Thompson House during the battle. There is some suggestion the house was a duplex, and as Mary was listed as the only resident of that dwelling in 1860, the other half of the house may have been unoccupied at the time of the battle, making it very convenient for Lee and his staff.[17] Shortly after the battle Michael Jacobs, a professor at Pennsylvania College, talked with Mrs. Thompson about the general's use of her house. His account of the battle was published in 1864 and cannot be quickly dismissed.

Confederate Commander Robert E. Lee (1807-1870).
ACHS.

On Wednesday evening, after our men had been compelled to fall back and retire to the Cemetery Hill, this house was within the Rebel lines. Occupying an elevated position from which the Federal lines could be seen with a field glass, and being at a safe distance from our guns, it was selected by General Lee and his staff as his headquarters. Here he lodged all night and took his meals....Mrs. Thompson testifies to the gentlemanly deportment of General Lee whilst in her house, but complains bitterly of the robbery and general destruction of her goods by some of his attendants.[18]

Martin L. Stoever, another Professor of Pennsylvania College, had a different view of General Lee's gentlemanly deportment. In a letter written to a friend on September 30, 1863, he wrote "this wicked rebellion has so hardened and corrupted its actors that they seem to have lost all honor and principle".

I also heard the woman, whose house he made his headquarters, say that he made her deliver up all the jellies and jams she had with three bottles of wine which she had herself made for medicinal purpose, without offering her any compensation. He, moreover, in her presence with an oath [said] that he intended to make the Yankees that day (Thursday) dance.[19]

Of course with the important events that were unfolding on July 2, and 3, 1863, Lee spent little time at his headquarters on Seminary Ridge. But the tents of his headquarters staff were located there, and incoming messages, sent to Lee from all over the field, would first arrive at that central location. At least one courier remembered that he "delivired messages from Gen. Lee at the house to Gen. Ewell and Gen. Johnston all during the 2nd day's battle."[20] Because of its location, the area around the Thompson House would also become an important Confederate artillery position during the final two days of the battle. Early on the morning of July 2nd two Confederate batteries (8 guns) under the command of Captain Willis J. Dance were placed in position on Seminary Ridge near this location. Captain David Watson's battery of four ten pound parrott rifles were "placed on the left of the railroad cut," not far from where Stewart's 4th U.S. Battery had been located just a short time earlier, and Captain Benjamin H. Smith's Battery of four three-inch rifles was positioned along the ridge "near the Seminary used as a Yankee hospital." At the start of hostilities on the second day, around 4 o'clock that afternoon, these guns "opened on the enemy's batteries, and continued the cannonade until about dark."[21] Along the ridge in support of these guns was the North Carolina brigade of General Junius Daniel. When the Southern artillery began its bombardment "the enemy's artillery opened in reply...and from that time until nearly dark the portion of the line occupied by" Daniel's Brigade "was subjected to a heavy fire, from which, owing to their exposed situation, they suffered much."[22]

Although July 2nd was the bloodiest day of the battle, and the Southerners did gain much ground, the fighting that evening ended indecisively. With the issue still unresolved on the morning of the third day, Lee felt compelled to launch yet another major attack against the Union line in an attempt to break it away from its strong defensive position. The assault that would finally be decided upon would involve more than 12,000 men, and would require the crossing of almost a mile of open fields. To better insure the success of this attack, it was decided that the Confederate artillery would soften up the Union position immediately before the advance. This would hopefully knock out some of the Union batteries on Cemetery Hill which could fire on the exposed Southern infantry. All through the morning and early afternoon of July 3rd the area around the Thompson House was a hub of activity, as the artillery was moved into position for the cannonade. The batteries of Captain Watson and Captain Smith were taken from their positions and moved down the ridge to a point south of the Hagerstown Road.[23] In their place were posted ten rifled guns from the battalion of Colonel Thomas H. Carter. These guns were placed "on the ridge on the right and left of the railroad cut."

> These three batteries had been ordered to fire, in conjunction with a large number of guns on their right, on a salient part of the enemy's line prior to the charge of the infantry. The effect of this concentrated fire on that part of the line was obvious to all. Their fire slackened, and finally ceased. It was feebly resumed from a few guns when Pickett's and Hill's troops advanced, but the most destructive fire sustained by these troops came from the right and left of this salient.[24]

In all, about 150 Confederate cannons fired at the Union position for almost two hours. A civilian recalled that "it seemed as if the heavens and earth were crashing together."[25] But the bombardment was not as effective as the Southern gunners had thought. The cannons that had been silenced along Cemetery Ridge had simply stopped firing to conserve their ammunition for the attack that everyone knew was coming, and the batteries that had been damaged were replaced by reserve artillery. The effectiveness of the Union artillery fire and the distance of the open ground that the Confederate infantry had to cross was too much for Robert E. Lee's Army of Northern Virginia, and Pickett's Charge, as it has come to be called, ended as a Southern disaster.

With the Confederate failure on July 3rd, Seminary Ridge was hurriedly converted into a defensive position. Lee was convinced that a Federal counterattack was inevitable. During the early morning hours of the 4th of July, Southern forces evacuated the town they had held for the last two and a half days, and formed behind a strong line of breastworks along the top of Seminary Ridge.[26] These earthworks ran the length of the ridge, from Oak Hill to the Emmitsburg Road. Two Napoleons of Captain Hupp's Virginia Battery, under the command of Lieutenant Charles B. Griffin, were placed in position just south of the railroad cut, directly in front of Mrs. Thompson's House.[27] With the retreat of the Rebels from the town, Northern troops marched into it. Barricades were thrown up along Gettysburg's western edge, and throughout the day skirmishing continued between the Yankees in town, and the Rebels along the ridge. Mrs. Thompson, who was on the ridge all this time was reported by Michael Jacobs as hearing a conversation between Lee and Stuart on that historic Fourth of July.

> Of General Stuart whom she saw and heard converse with Lee in her house, she describes him as a man rough in his manner and cruel and savage in his suggestions. She heard him urge upon Lee the propriety of shelling and

destroying the town of Gettysburg after they should leave it and if it should be occupied, as it was on Saturday, the 4th, by our troops, and of displaying the black flag. To all of this General Lee is said to have replied in the negative, saying that they had never done so before, and that he was not willing to make a beginning on the present occasion.[28]

The attack Lee was expecting never came, and on the evening of July 4, 1863, during a drenching rain, the Confederates started their long journey back to Virginia. The town of Gettysburg would never again be the same.

With the departure of the Army of Northern Virginia, Meade's army soon followed, leaving more than 20,000 wounded soldiers behind. Gettysburg became a large hospital, caring not only for the Northern wounded but also for the Southerners who were too badly injured to be moved. "By the sixth of July one hundred and seventy-three wounded officers and men were collected in the Seminary hospital" alone.[29] At different times during the battle, Seminary Ridge had been used as a Northern and Southern defensive position, and the grounds around the Thompson House were strewn with the debris of battle. A few weeks after the battle, the Reverend Doctor Samuel Simon Schmucker, president of the Lutheran Seminary, wrote of the considerable damage done to his institution.

M.B. Brady photo taken shortly after the battle showing Confederate prisoners in front of the breastworks along Seminary Ridge. These are the fortifications built by the Southern army on July 4, 1863 which appear on most contemporary maps. **ACHS.**

The house I occupy was most damaged. The Rebels having driven the occupants out on the first day of the battle, took possession of it themselves and their batteries being also planted in the immediate vicinity, it was unavoidably shattered by the Federal Artillery from Cemetery Hill. Thirteen cannon balls or shells pierced the walls and made holes several of which were from two to three feet in length and nearly as broad, window frames were shattered to pieces, sash broken around the yard and garden were nearly all leveled with the ground, as well as those around the entire Seminary lands. The Seminary edifice was perforated by several balls, and large portions [were] knocked out of the North East gable corner. There being also a crack in the wall extending over two stories. Dr. Krauth's dwelling also received some injury, though not of a very serious nature. The fences around the fields as well as those along the Seminary Avenue were destroyed, many of the rails and boards incorporated with the breastwork, others broken and others burned....[30]

The home of the Reverend Doctor Charles Philip Krauth adjoined the properties of James H. Thompson and his brother-in-law Samuel K. Foulk. Reverend Krauth and his family had been forced to flee from their home during the heavy fighting of the first day's battle. In a claim made after the war by his wife, Harriet B. Krauth, for damages to their personal property, an affidavit given by Hannah P. Foulk was included. It describes a visit that Hannah made to the Krauth House just a few days after the battle.

Mrs. Hannah P. Foulk, a respectable and credible citizen...doth say that her dwelling at the time of the Battle of Gettysburg was on a lot adjoining that of the residence of Rev. Dr. C.P. Krauth and his family; that she was frequently at his house before and immediately previous to the battle and went into it on Monday after the battle and found it vacated. And that she had been in it on Sunday (5th) while it was yet occupied as a hospital and saw that the rooms on [the] first floor were filled with wounded and a surgeon and a wounded officer upstairs; that she was familiar with the contents of the house when the battle began and saw their condition at its close. That everything that could be eaten was consumed. The beds had been brought down [from upstairs] and used for the wounded; that four good mattresses were ruined and carried away, including also blankets and quilts...a large quantity of carpeting and matting was destroyed...clothing, both gentlemen and ladies were all taken; the drawers and wardrobes having been broken and riffled....[31]

The problem of supplies, and of caring for this incredible number of wounded, was compounded by the large number of sight-seers who flocked into the town to visit sights such as Reverend Schmucker described. Shortly after the battle Sarah Broadhead wrote in her diary that "the town is as full as ever of strangers, and the old story of the inability of a village of twenty-five hundred inhabitants, overrun and eaten out by two large armies, to accommodate from ten to twelve thousand visitors, is repeated almost hourly."[32]

One of these visitors was famed photographer Mathew Brady. During his visit to Gettysburg, he and his assistants recorded approximately 30 views of what he considered the major sites of the battlefield.[33] On July 15, 1863, Brady found himself on Seminary Ridge in front of Widow Thompson's small stone house. Someone had pointed this house out as General Lee's headquarters and his crew soon exposed at least four negatives of it, one showing Brady and Mary Thompson herself in front of the stone dwelling. Eleven of the photographs taken by Brady on his Gettysburg visit appeared as woodcuts in the August 22, 1863, edition of *Harper's Weekly*. Included was a view of the Thompson House captioned "General Lee's Head-quarters." In the text that followed a correspondent for *Harper's* correctly predicted that although it was a "modest, unpretending" farmhouse in itself, it was "destined hereafter to be as famous and as great an object of curiosity to travelers, as the barn and mill at Waterloo."[34] This one event, more than any other, would catapult Mrs. Thompson and her stone house into the national limelight.

A woodcut of the Thompson House that appeared in the August 22, 1863 edition of Harpers Weekly. **Author's collection.**

This stereo view is one of the four views recorded by M.B. Brady and his assistants in front of the Thompson House on July 15, 1863. GLHM.

PART
VI

Early Visitation

In November of 1863, throngs of people again poured into the little town of Gettysburg, this time to be present at the dedication of the Soldier's National Cemetery. A correspondent for the New York *Times* reported that the town was so crowded that "every house keeper in Gettysburgh [*sic*] has opened a temporary hotel."

> People from all parts of the country seem to have taken this opportunity to pay a visit to the battle-fields which are hereafter to make the name of Gettysburgh immortal...the scenes of the late battles have been visited by thousands of persons from every loyal State in the Union and there is probably not a foot of the grounds that has not been trodden over and over again by reverential feet.[1]

With thousands of people touring the field, it is not surprising that many journeyed onto Seminary Ridge to see the stone house used as the headquarters of General Robert E. Lee. In a letter written on November 20, 1863, Mrs. Edmund A. Souder of Philadelphia, Pennsylvania, described a carriage ride she had taken over the battlefield. "In the afternoon [November 18th] we rode to Seminary Hill, and saw Lee's headquarters."[2] Another visitor was the Reverend Franklin Jacob Fogel Schantz, a former student of the Lutheran Theological Seminary, from Allentown, Pennsylvania, who traveled to the ceremony with his longtime friend, Dr. Dewees J. Martin. On the long journey to reach Gettysburg, they became acquainted with a number of men also on their way to the dedication. Among them were Mr. Hays, correspondent for the New York *Herald*, Mr. Davenport, correspondent for the New York *Tribune*, and Mr. Baldwin of Vermont. Arriving late on the evening of November 17, the men decided to visit the battlefield early the next morning. Reverend Schantz later wrote of his experience.

> On Wednesday morning [November 18], Mr. Baldwin, Mr. Hays, Mr. Davenport, Dr. Martin, and I hired a carriage and were driven over the battlefield. First to the site of the first day's battle....When we stopped at a small house near the Rail Road cut, in which house Gen. Lee had his quarters, we met the wife of the occupant of the house. One of the party asked her whether she had cooked for Gen. Lee during his stay at the house. The question was sufficient to fill her with indignation and to cause her to give a sharp reply to the inquirer whether she had not cooked for Gen. Lee.[3]

Mr. Hays and Mr. Davenport, who were in the same carriage with Reverend Schantz, also wrote of the visit to Lee's Headquarters. Their accounts are both very similar to that of Reverend Schantz, except that they were published within days of the event. The account written by Mr. Hays, which was accompanied by a very detailed map of the town, appeared in the November 20, 1863 edition of the New York *Herald*.

> For the last few days there has been a stream of visitors wandering over the battlefield, picking up mementos of all kinds, from pieces of shell to walnut branches to be converted into walking canes. The first place usually visited is Seminary Hill, on which stands the college, the theological school, and a school for young ladies. Just over the brow of the hill stands a low-roofed small stone house of ruinous aspect, the headquarters of the rebel General Lee. An old German woman, who was the matron of the domicile, answered to our inquiries and gave Lee a good character for his moral discourse and bearing; but she protested indignantly that she had cooked nothing for the rebels. Lee had his pick of good houses, but preferred this humble one. Quite contiguous to it are the premises of Hon. [Edward] M. McPherson. No willful damage was done to them or any other property at Gettysburg.[4]

Mr. Davenport, the correspondent of the New York *Daily Tribune*, gives his account of the same conversation, but with a little more detail. His account of the events that occurred on the morning of November 18, was published on November 21, 1863.

> Soon after breakfast we took a conveyance, and in company with a few friends started out, first upon the Chambersburg Road, upon which the Rebels first entered the town on Friday, June 26. Pushing straight out from the center of the village, or from the Diamond, as it is here called, from its peculiar shape, for perhaps the distance of a mile, we came to the house occupied by Gen. Lee as his headquarters. As we halted before the door, an old lady, some sixty years of age, who owned the property and resided therein, came forth to look at the party. After asking of her various questions with references to the manners and habits of her uninvited guests, one of the party asked if she cooked for the General during his stay. Drawing herself up for a moment, and eyeing very keenly her questioner, she replied in a manner and tone as indicative of just indignation as of patriotism, "No, I guess I didn't cook for any Rebel. They had to do their own cooking." I find that this very question of the General's meals was one which occasioned him [Lee] some considerable difficulty.[5]

All three of these accounts talk of the same conversation, and from the descriptions given, it seems that the Widow Thompson is the one being interviewed. It is unfortunate that more information is not given, but it does appear that all were in agreement that the house was the site of Lee's headquarters. It is interesting that all three of the accounts use some form of the word "indignant" to describe Mary's response to being asked whether she cooked for Lee or not. She does not say that Lee did not eat in her house, only that she did not cook for him. Today, in the Lee's Headquarter's Museum is the table on which Lee supposedly ate. A note attached to the table states the following:

This is the table which Gens Lee, Longstreet, Early, Ewell and Adj Taylor ate supper from the evening of July 1st 1863. Prepared by Mrs. James Thompson and served in this room.

Signed,
Alice Folk, Grand-daughter[6]

The Mrs. James Thompson referred to as preparing the meal for the Southern officers is Mrs. Mary Jane Arendt Thompson, the wife of Mary's son James, who was probably with Mary in the house during the battle. It makes perfect sense that living so close, and alone with her small child, she would find refuge with Mary.[7] It does seem unlikely that all the people mentioned in the statement would have eaten on the table, but Alice Foulk was indeed Mary's granddaughter. Her mother was Hannah Foulk, and she was 7 years old during the battle.[8]

Another early visitor to the stone house was Brigadier General Herman Haupt, a one time resident of Seminary Ridge, who in the fall of 1863 had just returned to private life, having previously served as chief of construction and transportation on the U.S. Military Railroads.[9]

Gen. Herman Haupt and daughter visited Gettysburg the fall after the battle. Gen. Haupt had lived and taught school here on Oak Ridge, and being greatly interested in the battle, in company with his daughter and Miss Sue Kurtz visited the Widow Thompson at the old stone house known as Lee's Headquarters. They questioned her about Gen. Lee, and she told them how well she remembered and would never forget General Lee sitting on a chair at a window she pointed to, reading his Bible.[10]

During the years following the battle Mrs. Thompson's house was accepted by everyone as the site of General Lee's Headquarters, and it appears in the earliest maps of the field denoted as such. In the late fall of 1863, John Bachelder published an isometric map of the battlefield, showing the positions of the troops during the three days of fighting, as well as all the important landmarks. The map, which was based on fieldwork done by Bachelder within weeks of the battle, designated the Thompson House as "Gen Lee's Hd Qt.s."[11] In 1864, two separate maps of the field (S. G. Elliot's Map and the Andrew Cross map) were published which indicate the Thompson House as Lee's Headquarters. It is interesting to note that all three of the aforementioned maps also clearly mark the location of the breastworks built by Confederate soldiers after the failure of "Pickett's Charge." In places these works could still be seen years after the battle. They ran north-south along Seminary Ridge, and passed directly between the Thompson and Dustman houses.[12]

There is some evidence to suggest that Mrs. Thompson did not like her new found fame, and that she left Gettysburg for a short time after the battle. Despite her popularity however, Mrs. Thompson remained poor, and still required the assistance of Thaddeus Stevens. In July of 1866 Stevens, who was then a congressman in Washington D. C., wrote to a friend in Gettysburg:

Mrs. Thompson, our excellent friend, returns to live among her friends in Gettysburg, where I hope she may live in peace many years. Fortune has left her without much means, but while I live and have the ability she must be well

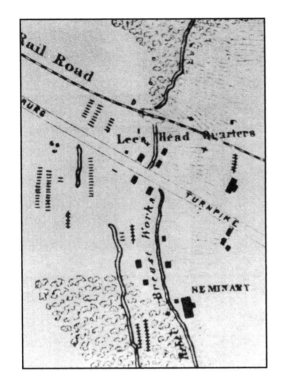

Detail of the 1864 Elliot map showing the area around the Thompson House. The hash marks on the map represent the sites of Union and Confederate graves. ALBG.

provided for. Will you take the trouble (I know you will gladly) to look after her comfort; when ever she needs money or any comforts please advance it to her and draw on me for the amount and I will immediately send it to you. I of course expect to aid none but her, but to treat all she desires with great liberality.[13]

Thaddeus Stevens died in 1868, and Mary Thompson lived out the rest of her life in the stone house on Seminary Ridge. She died of consumption and old age on May 25, 1873, and today is buried in Gettysburg's Evergreen Cemetery next to the graves of her son-in-law and daughter, Samuel K. and Hannah P. Foulk. She rests just a few feet from the location of the platform where Lincoln gave his immortal Gettysburg Address.[14]

On December 15, 1888, the stone house was sold at an auction to 41-year-old, Philip Hennig.[15] Hennig, who lived in town and owned a bakery on York Street, was born in Gettysburg. His brother had served in the Civil War, and during the battle his parents had cared for the wounded in their home on High Street.[16] He purchased the Thompson House for $740 as part of the estate of Thaddeus Stevens.[17] During the settlement of this estate, the executor, Edward McPherson, recorded the information from the sheriff's deed roll concerning the original sale of the property in 1846.

The grave of Mary Thompson in the Evergreen Cemetery, Gettysburg, Pennsylvania.

Benjamin Schriver, High Sheriff of Adams County, by his Deed Roll, executed and acknowledged January 28,1846 sold and conveyed the above named lot of ground in Cumberland Twp. to Thaddeus Stevens for the sum of $500.00. Said property being sold as the property of Michael Clarkson, Endorsed upon said sheriffs deed to Thaddeus Stevens is the following, "I hereby acknowledge that Thaddeus Stevens who purchased the property described in the within deed, the same in trust for me, only so far as he has received money to which I am entitled. Witness my hand and seal this 4 day of January 1846. Signed Mary X (her mark) Thompson. Witness, James A. Thompson and Benjamin Schriver.[18]

The sum of $500 glaringly appears in McPherson's transcription of the sheriff's deed roll, but there is little doubt that no such figure appears in the original, which can still be seen today in the Adams County Court House. McPherson was also directed by the court of Adams County to locate the heirs of Mrs. Thompson so that they might participate in the distribution of proceeds received from the sale of the house. In what appears to be a very carefully planned court proceeding, McPherson devised the following balance for the distribution of funds.

The amount of his private funds invested by Thaddeus Stevens, in the above real estate purchased by him as trustee aforesaid, January 28, 1846, was $140—

upon which sum interest is allowed from date of purchase to April 1, 1889 the date of confirmation of sale of said real estate under order of court.

Amount of purchase money paid by Thaddeus Stevens January 28, 1846 on said real estate.

said real estate.	140.00
Interest, 43 yrs. 2 mo. & 3 da.	362.60
Total	502.60[19]

That amount deducted from the almost $800 that had been derived from the sale and rent of the house, left the five remaining Thompson children with an inheritance of about $44 apiece.[20]

Even after the death of Mrs. Thompson, the house continued to attract visitors. During the first forty years after the battle, hundreds of monuments were dedicated on the fields around it, but none were erected by Southern states.[21] To many sightseers who came to visit the scene of the turning point of the American Civil War, the old stone house on Seminary Ridge became a monument in itself. The thousands of tourists who poured into Gettysburg year after year all wanted to see the legendary site of "Lee's Headquarters." Pictures were taken of it, and postcards showing the structure were sent all over the country.[22] One early souvenir booklet described it as "a picturesque little stone house," and noted that a tour of Gettysburg was "not deemed complete without a visit to that romantic structure."[23]

One of the earliest postwar accounts of a visit to the Thompson House appeared in a three volume pictorial history of the Civil War published in 1868. The author, Benson Lossing, toured a great number of battlefields shortly after the war,

GETTYSBURG, Pa.   Gen. Robert E. Lee,
his Headquarters and two Confederate Monuments.

Early 1900s postcard depicting the Confederate monuments on the battlefield at that time.

and sketched scenes that would later appear as engravings in his book. Lossing visited Gettysburg during the month of July 1863, and again in September 1866. On his second visit to the field, he made a sketch of the "Confederate Head-Quarters." In Volume III of his pictorial history of the Civil War, a map of the battlefield showed "Lee's H. Q." at the Thompson House, but the text described that Lee "made his head-quarters on Seminary Ridge, at the house of the venerable Mary Marshall, where the Chambersburg road crosses the eminence."[24] Since there is no record of anyone named Mary Marshall ever living in the area of Seminary Ridge, we can only assume that this is a mistake on the part of the writer. What is not a mistake however, is the drawing that Benson Lossing made of the Thompson House. As described in his own words "this was the appearance of Lee's headquarters when the writer sketched it, from the Chambersburg road, late in September, 1866. It was a substantial old stone house. Mrs. Marshall yet occupied it, and was then seventy-eight years of age."[25]

Another early account of a visit to the area is found in an article which appeared in the *Potter Journal* on September 18, 1879. It was part of a series of articles, written by a member of the 53rd Pennsylvania Volunteers, describing his return to the field after 16 years.

> We soon came to Seminary Ridge, along which the Rebels had their main line of works, extending from the Railroad cut south along the ridge to the Millerstown road. In many places these works are still to be seen. Here on the

Sketch of the Thompson House by Benson Lossing in September, 1866. GNMP.

height of ground, and where one has a fine view of the surrounding country, lives C. H. Dustman, a German, who lived here during the battle, and gave us many interesting accounts of it. His lot extends back to the Railroad cut. There was some hard fighting done here, as his buildings bear testimony. His house— a brick one—was used as a hospital on the first day; his barn has several holes through it, made by shot and shell. Just across the lane from Dustman's is a stone house, which is said to have been Gen. Lee's headquarters during the battle of Gettysburg, but this Dustman denies. He says Gen. Rambeau commanded this part of the Rebel line, and had his headquarters here, and that he afterwards had seen Gen. Lee here, but always on horseback. That his headquarters were back on the Chambersburg road. Dustman also spoils all the grand ideas you may have formed about the patriotism of John Burns, for he says he did no fighting at all; that he was merely out along the lines as a spectator, and had no gun at all; that he was wounded near his house; that he assisted in getting him home. But be that as it may, Burns had some courage to be about along the line.[26]

In 1863 Casper Henry Dustman was a 55 year old bootmaker, and lived with his large family, in the house adjacent to Mary's on Seminary Ridge.[27] The General Rambeau that is referred to is probably General Ramseur, whose troops did fight in that area during the first day of the battle. On the second and third day his troops were positioned at the other end of town facing Cemetery hill, and it is unlikely that his headquarters would have been so far from his brigade. There are numerous first hand accounts to verify that John Burns did have a gun in his hand, and fought side-by-side Northern troops of the "Iron Brigade" on July 1, 1863. It is not known why Dustman was trying to refute the legends of John Burns and the Widow Thompson, but it is important to note that this is the first documented incident of someone questioning the location of the Thompson House as the site of Lee's headquarters.

In February 1895 an act was passed through Congress "to establish a National Military Park at Gettysburg," and shortly thereafter, the Gettysburg Battlefield Memorial Association (GBMA) turned over its grounds and monuments to the Federal Government. In the official history of the GBMA, written by one of its directors and first published in 1897, "a brief but accurate account of the battle" is included. Among the many illustrations is a photograph of the Thompson House entitled "Lee's Headquarters." The text specifies that "Lee's Headquarters was in the brick house, on the Chambersburg Road, in the rear of and near the seminary."[28] This being its official history, we must assume that the GBMA recognized this house as the official site of Lee's Headquarters. At this point, it probably looked as if the Thompson House was destined to be one of America's great historic sites, but the story does not end there; controversy was looming.

Part VII

Controversy

On the night of August 26, 1896, the Thompson House, while under the ownership of Philip Hennig, caught fire and the inside of the structure was completely gutted. At the time, the tenants of the house, James McLaughlin and Mrs. Emma Feister, were not at home, but they lost almost all their possessions in the fire. Luckily, Hennig had insurance on the historic structure, and was able to rebuild the dwelling just as it was "in order to preserve a battlefield relic."[1] An article that appeared in the Gettysburg *Compiler* the following week tells of the fire, but this item in the newspaper is important for another reason. For the first time we read of a movement to discredit the Thompson House as the location of Lee's Headquarters.

An 1860s photo of Philip Hennig (1847–1918). He purchased the Thompson House at an auction in 1888 and owned the house until his death. (ACHS)

The article states that "though popular tradition has it that this building was used by General Lee as his headquarters during the Battle of Gettysburg, there seems to be considerable doubt as to the fact." It then goes on to give the opinions of a number of guides, and civilians concerning the matter. William D. Holtzworth (Guide), Henry Dustman (nephew of Casper Dustman), Col. John Nicholson (Park Commissioner), Luther W. Minnigh (Guide), and Captain James T. Long (Guide) were the men whose names are given as being consulted. It is important to remember that in this article, the dispute centered around whether Lee had used the house as his official headquarters, and not whether Lee was ever inside the Thompson House itself. In fact, Luther Minnigh stated "that Mrs. Thompson, who lived in the stone house on Seminary Ridge told him that General Lee was in the house" for a short time. Only Dustman claimed that Lee was never in the house, stating that his uncle (Casper Dustman) had told him that several times, and it could be "corroborated by a lady who lived within a hundred feet of the building." But there was no name given to this "lady" and it is not known to whom Dustman was referring. It is also interesting to note, that while these men were quick to dismiss the Thompson House as the site of Lee's Headquarters, the speculation as to the actual site varied. Minnigh thought the site was in the apple orchard owned by Samuel Hartzell. Captain Long stated that he thought "Lee had no established headquarters, but occupied headquarter tents which were moved from time to time," and Holtzworth, who was deceased at the time of the article, was quoted as saying that Lee had no established headquarters at all during the battle.[2] Over the next few years this discussion over where Lee's official headquarters were located would steamroll, and by the turn of the century, there were many who disputed the fact that Lee ever placed a foot inside the Thompson House. Although most of these stories were based on conjecture and were often told by people not present at the battle, over the years many writers and historians have put more credence in these secondary sources than in the first hand accounts written during and shortly after the Civil War.

The next mention of the Thompson House in the local papers came on June 5, 1907, when it was announced that 53 year old Emaline Feister, a long time resident of Lee's Headquarters, was arrested and charged "with keeping a bawdy house and place for the practice of fornication to the common nuisance and disturbance of the neighborhood."

> The talk about the house has been such that battlefield guides have not pointed it out because of explanations that might be made necessary if a visit to Lee's Headquarters was suggested. It is to be hoped that this historical landmark can be so restored as to be pointed to and visited by those interested in the battlefield.[3]

With all the problems going on at the old stone house, it was no wonder that people would rather not designate it as an historic site. And during this period, while other significant tracts of land were being purchased by the War Department, and included in the park boundary, the Thompson House would be passed over. There can be no doubt that this bad press is one of the reasons this site has continued to remain in private hands.

Lee's Headquarters, from a 1903 "Gettysburg" souvenir booklet.

Also in 1907 came the most serious attack against the Thompson House when Henry S. Moyer, from Allentown, Pennsylvania, published an article entitled, "Where Were General Lee's Headquarters at Gettysburg?" The article, which originally appeared in the *Pennsylvania German Magazine*, was reprinted in the Gettysburg *Compiler* on March 30, 1910. Moyer's study of the controversy regarding Lee's Headquarters has been cited by historians, over and over again, as proof that Lee did not occupy the Thompson House. But in reality the account provides us with very little new information. Most of his article is filled with accounts suggesting that Lee "was adverse to having better quarters than his own soldiers, and time and time again refused...to be better cared for than his troops."[4] He very seldom located his headquarters in any structure other than his tent, and therefore could not have possibly used the Thompson House. To understand this argument, one has to realize that by the turn of the century Robert E. Lee had been elevated to a god-like status in the South, and it is quite possible that the Southern officers who agreed with Moyer were doing so solely to protect the general's image.

The strongest piece of evidence presented by Moyer is an interview which he supposedly had with a resident of the house on Seminary Ridge designated as Lee's Headquarters. Moyer stated that in "the spring of 1874" he traveled to Gettysburg to visit his good friend and associate, Philip C. Croll, who was then attending Pennsylvania College.[5] During his stay he toured the battlefield, and as he had "always entertained an exalted opinion of General Robert E. Lee" was most anxious to visit the spot where his headquarters were located.

I was directed to the modest house...which stands on the crest of Seminary Ridge, north of the Chambersburg Pike. It was on one of those beautiful early April mornings when the earth seems to make an effort to rejuvenate itself. On entering the yard I found an old lady sitting on the porch, enjoying the morning sunlight. To me she appeared to be about eighty years old, yet well preserved. After the usual salutation and self introduction, I asked her if she had any objection to answer a few questions upon which I was seeking information. She told me that it would be a pleasure for her to give me any information she could. The following were the questions asked and the answers given:

1. Did you occupy this house on July 1, 1863? "Yes sir." Some of the neighbors told me that all fled when the battle began, so I made the second question more specific.

2. Did you occupy this house the whole of July, 1, 1863? "Yes sir, I never left it."

3. Did General Lee have his headquarters in this house? "No sir."

4. Are you sure that General Lee was never in this house? "Yes sir, I can positively assure you that General Lee was never in this house."

I did not doubt the old lady's word then, nor have I done so since, as there was no occasion for it. The answers were given in a straightforward and dignified manner. This appears to me sufficient proof that General Lee did not have his headquarters in the house that has been designated as such.[6]

Moyer does not give the name of the "old lady" he talked with 30 years earlier, but there is a strong inference that it was Mrs. Thompson. However, no such interview could have taken place in the spring of 1874, because Mary Thompson had died a year earlier.[7] Within a few months of the article's appearance in the Gettysburg newspaper, Moyer was forced to admit that he did not know the identity of the "old lady" he had interviewed and was not sure if it was Mrs. Thompson. But, he still contended that the lady he talked with was the resident of the house during the battle. Clouding the issue further, he added that it was the "people in the community" who "persisted in saying that the Widow Thompson occupied the house at the time of the battle," while Benson Lossing recorded her name as Mary Marshall.[8] The likelihood that Moyer was referring to another "old lady" that lived in that house is very slim. The evidence is overwhelming that Mary Thompson was indeed the occupant of the house on Seminary Ridge, and besides her children, the records do not indicate that anyone else ever lived with Mary in that stone house, before, during, or after the battle.

Of all the information in Moyer's article, by far the most interesting and most controversial is something that "Col. Bachelder said to a good friend of the writer."

After the war I had an interview with General Lee, and among other matters discussed was the question where his headquarters were at the battle of Gettysburg. General Lee answered in the following words: "My headquarters were in tents, in an apple orchard, back of the seminary along the Chambersburg pike."[9]

Once again, he is quoting a conversation that supposedly took place 30 years earlier. According to Moyer, "a good friend" had at some point talked with former Government Historian, John B. Bachelder, and during that conversation Bachelder told him of an interview that had taken place with Robert E. Lee before he died. It is interesting to note that the friend who gave this information to Moyer is also unnamed. John Bachelder, who is well known for gathering hundreds of accounts from participants of the battle, died in 1894, and despite the voluminous papers he left behind, there is no documentation that suggests he ever interviewed Robert E. Lee.[10] It is not known why Henry Moyer would fabricate these exaggerated claims, but without them, his article becomes nothing more than his opinion.

On August 3, 1910, an article appeared in the Gettysburg *Compiler* written by Vina C. Weirick, in response to Moyer. She agreed wholeheartedly that the house of "old lady Thompson" was not used by Lee, but argued a totally different location for the actual site. Weirick's article is quite lengthy and seems to ramble on for paragraphs, but she does have some interesting things to say. She lived in Gettysburg during the battle, and was a student of Miss Carrie Sheads' Oak Ridge Seminary.

> General Lee's headquarters were included in the space, between Oakridge Seminary, and the hill, including the house occupied by some one, named Marshall. There is an apple orchard in that space, but not an extensive one. And there may have been some other trees, also. And there was a lot of grass, as that apple orchard was not kept with the neatness apple orchards are now kept. There were tents pitched there during the battle, and I heard those tents referred to, as the Headquarters of General Lee. Some of the young ladies, the Baltimore girls particularly, and I can name them, were in the Oakridge Seminary, during the Battle, and assisted the wounded who were taken there, as you can learn. And afterwards, we talked about the terrible scenes of the Battle, and General Lee being so near them. He may have been also, in the house at the top of the hill, as mention was made, in a commiserating way, as we "talked" of the aged lady living there before the Battle, and she must have been there during the Battle, as she was blind, or partially so. And if the links in the chain could be connected, perhaps the statement, or reply of the "old lady" Thompson, who lived in the now "said house" would be better understood, and the truth made plain.[11]

Even though it appears that Mrs. Weirick felt very strongly about this issue, there is no other documentation to support her arguments. It seems unlikely that Lee would have set his headquarters tents on the east side of Seminary Ridge, in plain view of, and within easy range of, Union artillery on Cemetery Hill. She is also confused as to the identity of the Mrs. Marshall described by Moyer, and is willing to admit that Lee's Headquarters may have included her house, but not Mrs. Thompson's. From her statements it is clear that Mrs. Weirick did not realize that the house referred to as Mrs. Marshall's by Moyer and Lossing, is the identical house referred to as the Thompson House by everyone else.

In 1911 Henry S. Moyer printed his article concerning Lee's Headquarters as a small four page pamphlet. Among the changes made to his original article was the

1880s Tipton photo of the Thompson House. **ACHS.**

deletion of the line relating how Moyer had learned through a friend, of the interview that Bachelder had with Lee. In this publication the quote from General Lee concerning his headquarters is printed as if it were copied down from some document to which he had access.[12]

As a result of this bad publicity we can only assume Philip Hennig, the owner of the house was anxious to acquire some documentation of his own. During the fiftieth anniversary of the battle in 1913, the opportunity presented itself in the form of Confederate veterans attending the reunion. Exactly what transpired is not known, but the following documents were the result.

Gettysburg Pa
July 2, 1913

I placed 4 guard around the old stone house on the hill, the personal headquarters of Gen Lee the evening of July 1 1863 about 5.30 p.m, at the command of Adj. Gen. Taylor, who was in the field headquarters across the street in a tent with Col. Douglas. I delivired messages from Gen Lee at the house to Gen. Ewell and Gen Johnston all during the 2 days battle.

Sgt M. T. Gander
39 Bat. Gen R E Lee
Courier and Scout
Luray, Va

Attached to the document is a slip of paper on which is inscribed in crude handwriting: "Gbg. 7/2 Sargent Martin V. Gander 39 Batalion Gen R. E. Lee. Courreier and Scouts. I am 86 years old."[13]

Although the authenticity of this document has been disputed over the years, records at the National Archives indicate that Martin V. Gander was indeed a sergeant of Co. C, 39th Virginia Cavalry Battalion, was present during the battle, and enlisted at Luray, Virginia. Records also clearly indicate that this company was used as "Scouts, Guides and Couriers" for Lee and his staff during the Gettysburg Campaign.[14] A second affidavit was apparently taken at the same time, and in the same handwriting as the first.

50th Anniversary, Gettysburg, Pa
July 2, 1913

> I was a courier on Adj Gen Taylors Staff at Gettysburg, July 1,2,3, 1863. I was dispatched to Gen Early east of village to notify him to appear at Gen Lee's H'd'qr's west of villiage in an old stone house for a council at 7.45 P.M. July 1, 1863 order Adj Taylor

Per Gen R.E. Lee

Written at the bottom of this slip of paper is a signature which is so hard to read that it has precluded any identification of the individual who gave it. The best guess is that it reads F. S. Gore (last name unrecognizable), 14 Lt Inp. (or La Art.), Longstreets Corps.[15] Although there would seem to be little reason to question the authenticity of these documents, it is the existence of a third similar affidavit that has called them both into question.

Hagerstown, Md
July 26, 1913

> I was in the Confederate Army and was attached to Gen. R. E. Lee's staff at Gettysburg. I was located in an apple orchard along the pike near a little white house, my tent being used by adj. Gen. Taylor and Gen. Lee to inspect maps in. I had the door of the stone house across the street, where Gen. Lee and staff ate meals and held councils of war, the door was used as a map table.

Col. Henry Kyd Douglas
Hagerstown, Md.[16]

There are several problems with this document, not the least of which is that Henry K. Douglas was dead at the time it was supposedly written. It is very hard to explain how or why this document originated. Over the years many have concluded that someone was purposely trying to deceive the public. But if that is true, why does the statement not go into more detail, or emphatically state that Lee did use the house as his headquarters? It seems that the emphasis is on the door of the stone house, and not the headquarters controversy. Today the documents remain shrouded in mystery. The authenticity of one can be easily documented, while the credibility of another is easily called into question. One would conclude that the documents have no relationship to each other whatsoever if it were not for the fact that Martin Gander mentions Douglas in his account.[17]

On June 8, 1917, a ceremony was held along Seminary Ridge, overlooking the fields of Pickett's immortal charge. Thousands of visitors watched as the Virginia Memorial became the first Confederate state monument dedicated on the entire field. Surmounted by an equestrian statue of General Robert E. Lee, it cost an estimated $50,000. The day after the event, a story ran on the front page of the Gettysburg *Times* entitled "Lee's Servant Here on Friday." A reporter for the *Times* who was mingling in the crowd at the dedication happened upon two men who actually claimed to have been servants of Lee during the war. The men, who were identified only as "old Negro servants," talked very fondly of the commanding officer.

> Among other things asked of the visitors was the question regarding the location of Lee's Headquarters during the battle. The Old Negro spoke emphatically on this subject and said that the place was in the field west of the Seminary Ridge, and south of the Chambersburg Pike. This verifies the inscription on the tablet along the road and adds weight to the contention of those who argue the old stone house never was used as his headquarters.
>
> That the building was occupied by General Lee for a short time during the three days was conceded as possible by the Negro. But he insisted that this was only temporary, that his main headquarters were in the field, and that there was where General Lee stayed when he was not engaged somewhere else directing the battle.[18]

Again, the argument is not whether Lee ever occupied the Thompson House, but whether it was his headquarters or not. It is also obvious that the writer of this article is trying to lead the reader to the conclusion that the stone house was not used. It looks as if the servant did in fact tell the reporter that the Thompson House was used by Lee in some capacity, but that part of his statement seems to be downplayed. It is unfortunate that the reporter did not think it important to give the names of the servants so that this story could be better verified. From this article we do learn however, that as early as June 1917, there was a "tablet along the road" marking the location of Lee's Headquarters as being just opposite the Thompson House on the south side of the road.[19] By 1919 the Gettysburg National Park Commission had erected a permanent marker, establishing Lee's Headquarters as being across the road from the Thompson House.[20] This marker is a bronze upright cannon barrel in a block of cement, on which is a plaque with the inscription:

> "MY HEAD QUARTERS WERE IN TENTS IN AN APPLE ORCHARD BACK OF THE SEMINARY ALONG THE CHAMBERSBURG PIKE" ROBT. E. LEE. The citation on the monument may sound familiar; it is the quote from Moyer's article.[21]

With the death of Philip Hennig in 1918, the house passed to his widow and was eventually sold to Clyde F. Daley on July 13, 1921.[22] Shortly after his purchase an article appeared in the local paper.

Headquarters of General Lee Sold. Repairs are underway on the building just west of the borough limits on Buford street, known as the headquarters of General Lee during the battle of Gettysburg, by C. F. Daly [*sic*], manager of the Five and Ten Cent Store, who recently purchased the property and the one across the Lincoln Highway from it, from Mrs. Susan Henning. Mr. Daly [*sic*] will open a curio and souvenir shop in the front of the building. His family will move there next spring.[23]

(Above) Postcard of the "Lee Museum" under Clyde Daley's ownership. Note the dormers, apparently added when the stone house was reconstructed after the fire.

(Below) Advertisement in the 75th Anniversary Edition (July 1938) of the Gettysburg *Times.*

LEE MUSEUM

C. F. Daley, Proprietor and Guide

Personal Headquarters of

General Lee

TOURIST	BATTLEFIELD
CABINS	SOUVENIRS

View of the inside of General Lee's Headquarters Museum ca. 1950, before the museum was remodeled. **Williams Collection, ACHS.**

Daley, not originally from Gettysburg, was 40 years old at the time of the purchase. By those who remember him, he is described as a "Short, feisty, Irishman." Sometime before 1920 he married Miriam F. Trimmer, the daughter of Samuel, who owned Trimmer's Five and Ten Cents Store. It was Daley who first opened the Thompson House to the general public. He originated "Lee Campground," building a bath house, and long cottage which he divided into rooms for overnight travelers. A room on the southwest corner of the stone house was used as a "curio and souvenir shop" and the rest of the structure as his residence.[24] At some point he amassed a large collection of battlefield relics, which are still on display at the museum today. Early into his ownership, Daley began to solicit information regarding the Thompson House, and collect objects related to it. Much of the information used in this book was made possible through his efforts.[25] In 1945 Daley sold the property to Eric F. Larson and retired to Florida.[26]

Larson, born in Sweden, had moved with his family to Gettysburg years earlier and purchased the Dustman House, which they converted into a tourist home. Larson, who worked as a carpenter and licensed battlefield guide, converted Daley's campground into Larson's Cottage Court and in 1953 formed the Larson Corporation. Over the years the motel has expanded, and "General Lee's Restaurant" is now situated on the spot where the Dustman House once stood, but Lee's

Larson's Cottage Court ca. 1950. **Williams Collection, ACHS.**

Headquarters Museum still stands just as it did when Daley first opened it in 1921.[27] It now encompasses four rooms of the stone house, and though its ownership has recently changed, it contains most of Daley's original collection.

The official National Park Service position is that Lee's headquarters was established in a small tent on the south side of the Chambersburg Pike, along with the tents of his staff officers and aides, and not in the Widow Thompson's stone house. But regardless of where his headquarters tent may have been located, there are first hand accounts that place him inside the house itself. Even if one ignores the fact that Lee occupied the structure at some point during the battle, there was still plenty of serious fighting that occurred there. It seems almost mind-boggling that the stone house and the ground around it were never purchased by the park. The Thompson House, the railroad cut, and "the gauntlet" represent the site of the heaviest fighting of the entire Battle of Gettysburg which is not included in the current park boundary.

The explanation for this is long and complicated, and can be traced back to the organization of the battlefield park itself. Gettysburg is a military park organized by Northern veterans, in a Northern state. Of the over 1400 monuments, markers, and tablets on the Gettysburg Battlefield, only about 20 were erected by Southerners. By the year 1900, most of the Northern regimental monuments had already been erected, and it was not until later that the War Department would erect the bronze plaques that now designate the positions of Southern brigades.[28] The collapse of the Federal position around the Thompson House was the worst Union defeat during the battle, and the railroad cut was the site of the largest mass capture of Northern soldiers during the entire three days at Gettysburg. In the minds of the Union veterans the least said about this site, the better.

The early documentation clearly shows that Lee established his headquarters in the house, or within a few feet of it, depending on which view you accept. It was not until 40 years after the battle that accounts began to surface which discredit the house as the site of the headquarters. These later accounts were based mostly on hearsay and no contemporary documentation. Nonetheless, within the last fifty years, historians and Park Service officials alike, have put more credence in the accounts of people such as Henry S. Moyer, than in the accounts of people who were actually there. If attitudes are not soon changed, we may one day lose this important landmark. Even though the ground around it has changed dramatically, the Thompson House still stands. And like the hundreds of other stone monuments that are scattered around the battlefield, it has its own distinctive story to tell.

Appendix

The Descendants of Mary Thompson

As already discussed, much of the myth and legend surrounding the story of Lee's Headquarters deals with the "Widow Thompson" herself. During the research conducted for this study, many of the nagging questions surrounding the Thompson House were only answered after gathering a large amount of material relating to the family of Mary Thompson and families of her children. During this project, I was fortunate enough to talk with many of Mary's direct descendants, and was provided with much valuable data through my correspondence with them. I was also given the priviledge (albeit honorary) of becoming a member of the Thompson Family Association. Because of the information I have been able to gather, together with that I obtained from members of the Thompson family, we now have a much better understanding of the life of "Widow Thompson" and the whereabouts of her descendants. Most helpful in this research have been R. William Bean of Urbana, Ohio (descendant of Elias Thompson), and Evelyn D. Hughes of Lewisberry, Pennsylvania (descendant of Hannah P. Thompson Foulk). The following list of descendants is incomplete, but is provided here in the hopes that it will lead to the discovery of more information concerning the Thompson Family.

Mary was born on November 12, 1793 in Germany Township, York County (now Adams County), Pennsylvania. Her parents were Philip Leopold Long ,or Lang, (1747-1832) and Phillipina Henning Long (1755-1821). She was baptized at the St. John Evangelical Lutheran Church of Littlestown, Pa. on March 8, 1794 as Ann Marie Long. She was one of at least seven children. During her 79 years Mary would outlive two husbands, and bare eight children. She died on May 25, 1873, and was buried shortly after in the Evergreen Cemetery at Gettysburg, Pa.

About 1818 Mary Long was married to Daniel Sell (Ca. 1792-1822). They had three children together. While little is known concerning Daniel Sell, it does seem he was born in Pa. and died in Md. prior to the birth of his third child.

1. **Eliza Sell (1820-).**
    Married in 1855 to Henry Long (1821-). Both Henry and Mary were born in Pa. The couple moved to Missouri sometime around the outbreak of the Civil War.

    Children:
    Mary S. Long (1862-).
    In the 1900 Census both Eliza and Henry were still living near Gallatin, Daviess Co., Missouri. No other information is known about this line of the family, but it is rumored that Henry Long fought in the Confederate army during the war.

2. **Hannah Phillipina Foulk (1821-1899).**
Hannah was born in Md. She was married at Gettysburg, Pa. in 1850 to Samuel Klineyoung Foulk (1827-1913). They died in Adams Co., and are buried in the Evergreen Cemetery at Gettysburg, Pa.
Children:
David Ziegler Foulk (1853-1915). Never Married. Graduate of the Gettysburg College (1871) and Gettysburg Lutheran Seminary (1873). Died in Adams Co., Pa.
Anna M. Foulk (1854-1931). Never Married. Died in Adams Co., Pa.
Alice Johnetta Foulk (1856-1923). Never Married. Died in Adams Co., Pa.
Samuel Norvel Foulk (1859-1942). Never Married. Died in Adams Co., Pa. Sarah Elizabeth Foulk (1861-1910). Married in Adams Co., Pa in 1889 to Benjamin Franklin Eichelberger (1859-1940). Died in York Co., Pa.

> *Children:*
> Ivan Daniel, Percy Samuel, Hannah Sell, Benjamin William, Elmer Elsworth, Elmira, John Luther, and Clyde Jacob Eichelberger.

Descendants of Hannah Foulk, who remained closer to her mother than any of the other children, have always been conscious of their relationship to Lee's Headquarters. Valuable information concerning Mary Thompson was gathered by members of the Foulk line. Ironically, it was not until this study that members of the Foulk family in Pa. learned of their Thompson family relatives in Ohio.

3. **Mary Jane Sell (1823-).**
Married in Adams Co., Pa. in 1842 to Jacob Shroder Carey (1813-1903). Both Jacob and Mary were born in Adams Co., Pa. They moved to Ohio in 1853. Most likely they both died in Champaign Co., Ohio.

Children:
Ann Carey (1844-). Born in Adams Co., Pa.
John Henry Carey (1845-). Born in Adams Co., Pa.
Daniel S. Carey (1846-). Born in Adams Co., Pa. Married Maria.
Eliza A. Carey (1848-). Born in Adams Co., Pa.
Mary E. Carey (1850-). Born in Adams Co., Pa.
Alice C. Carey (1852-). Born in Adams Co., Pa.
Jacob E. Carey (1854-). Born in Ohio.
James W. Carey (1858-). Born in Ohio.
Benjamin N. Carey (1861-). Born in Ohio.
Charles L. Carey (1863-). Born in Ohio.
Martha M. Carey (1867-). Born in Ohio.

With the large number of children that were born to Jacob and Mary, one can only imagine the number of Mary Thompson descendants that now live in Champaign Co., Ohio. It is hoped that some of these relatives may still have information that could help us better understand the story of Mary's first husband, Daniel Sell.

About 1826 Mary Sell married Joshua F. Thompson (ca. 1805-1850). As is the case with Mary's first husband, Joshua's parents are not known, but it is almost certain that he was born in Pa. The exact date and place of his death has also remained a mystery. Five more children were born to Mary during their marriage.

4. **James Henry Thompson (1827-1908).**
Married about 1858 to (lst) Mary Jane Arendt (1840-1869), and in 1872 to (2nd) Elizabeth Routson (1834-), widow of Benjamin Whitmore of Md. Both James and Mary were born in Adams Co., Pa. Shortly afterhis second marriage James and his family moved to Missouri, then to Pittsburgh, and finally settled in Champaign Co., Ohio where James died. He is buried in New Philadelphia Cemetery, Logan Co., Ohio.

Children by Mary Jane Arendt:
Elias Frederick Thompson (1859-1938). Born in Adams Co., Pa. Married to (lst) Margaret Jane Reprogle, and (2nd) Della Downing Philip.
> *Children:* Ada May, Lloyd, Lawrance Elias, Hugh Otto, and George Leonard Thompson.

Jane Meade Thompson (1863-1864). Jane was born on June 30, 1863, one day prior to the battle. She would die of inflammation of the lungs just eight months and nine days later on March 8, 1864. She died in Adams Co. and is buried in the Evergreen Cemetery in Gettysburg, Pa. next to her mother, Mary Jane.

Anna Louise Thompson (1865-). Born in Adams Co., Pa. Married John Thomas Keating.
> *Children:* Wilbur, Andrew, Micheal, Mildred, Flossie, and Thomas Keating.

Eleanora Thompson (1867-). Born in Adams Co., Pa. Married Oscar Murphy.

Children by Elizabeth:

Gertrude Anastasia Thompson (1869-1947). Born in Frederick Co., Md. Married David Austin Hale.
> *Children:* Ida, William Harrison, Lula, David F. Hale.

Maggie Thompson (ca.1869-1875). Born in Frederick Co., Md. Maggie and Gertrude were twins.

Josie Thompson (ca. 1873-1875).

5. **Elias Thompson (1828-1914).**
Married in Champaign Co., Ohio in 1854 to Mary Ann Hunter (1834-1903). Elias moved from Pa. to Ohio about 1853. He died in Logan Co. and is buried in the Fairview Cemetery, West Liberty, Ohio.

Children:
William H. Thompson (1855-1921). Married to Eva A. Died in Champaign Co., Ohio.

Berthina E. (1858-). Married to David M. Payne.
> *Children:* Harry and Walter Payne.

Mary E. Thompson (1861-1937). Married to Samuel M. Braumiller. Died in Clarke Co., Ohio.

> *Children:* Bessie and William Braumiller

John Harrison Thompson (1863-1938). Married to (lst) Lilly May Rickets (-1888), and Dora Belle Newsom (1870-1934). Died in Champaign Co., Ohio.

> *Children:* Herman Stanley, Maude Beatrice, Nellie Marie, Bertha Elizabeth, Paul N., Raymond L., and William E. Thompson.

Lydia J. Thompson (1865-). Married to Harry Ward. Died in Champaign Co., Ohio.

Amos Elias Thompson (1868-1940). Never married. Died in Champaign Co., Ohio.

Clara Della Thompson (1874-1940). Married to David Culp.

> *One child:* Ross Culp.

Much more information is available concerning the descendants of James and Elias Thompson. If you are interested in learning more, please contact the Thompson Family Association, whose address is included at the end of this section.

Elias Thompson (1829-1914) and his family. Standing in back from Left to Right are; William H., Berthina E., and John Harrison Thompson. Seated in Middle row are; Elias, Mary Ann (Hunter), Clara Della, and Amos Elias Thompson; and seated in front of them are Mary E. and Lida J. Thompson. **Photo Courtesy of R. William Bean.**

6. Catherine Sarah Thompson (1830-1904).
Married John Yohn (1831-1869). John and Catherine were both born in Pa. Both moved to Ohio where they were married and all their children were born. After John's death, Catherine moved back to Gettysburg, Adams Co., Pa. were she died. She is buried in the Evergreen Cemetery, Gettysburg, Pa.

Children:
Amos S. Yohn (1860-). Born in Ohio.
George B. Yohn (1862-). Born in Ohio.
Mary Eliza Yohn (1864-1938). Born in Ohio. She moved back to Adams Co. with her mother and married James Buchanan Crist.
>*Children:* Effie Margaret Esther (married William Ensor), Bernice, John W., Kermit, and an unnamed daughter (Mrs. John Clem of Fort Wayne, Indiana).

John W. Yohn (1866-1939). Born in Ohio. Never Married. Died in Adams Co., Pa.
Ida May Yohn (1868-). Born in Ohio. Married to a man named Clem. In 1938 they were recorded as living in St. Paris, Champaign Co., Ohio.

The family of Catherine Sarah (Thompson) Yohn is most intriguing, for although there must still be a large number of her direct descendants living in Adams County, Pa., the author has not as yet met one. It is hoped that with the publication of this book that new information will come to light from this line of the family.

7. Margaret Isabella Thompson (1834-).
Married a man named Barnett who was apparently from Kansas.

Children:
Joshua L. Barnett (1865-). Born in Illinois.
Jacob A. Barnett (1869-). Born in Ohio.

At present there is little to go on concerning this part of the family, but it is probable that Barnett's still live in Champaign Co., Ohio who are related to Mary Thompson.

8. Susannah Thompson (1836-).
Married in 1855 to Napoleon Sowers (1835-). Susannah was born in Pa., but Napoleon was born in Virginia.

Children:
Charles C. Sowers (1856-). Born in Adams Co., Pa.
William Sowers (1857-). Born in Adams Co., Pa.
Mary A. Sowers (1859-). Born in Adams Co., Pa.

This Sowers family information was taken from the 1860 Census for the Borough of Gettysburg. They disappear from the records soon after and at present nothing else is known about this line of the family.

The Story of Lee's Headquarters: Update

Since the publication of my book, I have uncovered quite a number of other interesting sources pertaining to *The Story of Lee's Headquarters*. For the interest of the reader I have here included two of my latest finds, the most important of which is an article printed in the *Lutheran and Missionary* (a Philadelphia newspaper) on September 24, 1863. This is the earliest known interview with the widow and is compelling evidence that Lee did use the Thompson House in some capacity during the battle.

THE REBEL GENERAL IN CHIEF - We have noticed in some of our journals unfavorable statements respecting the personal bearing of General Lee. It is pleasant to be able to cite the following, which is given by a correspondent of the *Sunday School Times* writing from the field of Gettysburg:

A day or two ago we went to call on Mrs. Thompson, whose house it is said General Lee occupied as his headquarters. Dr. Junkin had heard that Mrs. Thompson had stated that Lee frequently used profane language while at her house. He wished to hear the statement from her own lips; and for this purpose we went in company to see her.

She states that Lee occupied her house from Wednesday evening, July 1st, until Friday night, and that she never heard any profane or improper language from him. General Stuart was with him part of the time. The impression which she had of him was not favorable. Stuart wanted to enter Gettysburg, and burn and make an indiscriminate plunder of all property, but to this Gen. Lee would not consent. She thought Stuart was a bad man; but Lee expressed himself and acted like a humane man showing much feeling on account of the sufferings and the horrors of War.

A tourist to Gettysburg in 1926 paid a visit to "Lee Museum" while it was under the ownership of Clyde Daley, and gave the following interesting description. It was printed in *Confederate Veteran*, Vol. 34 (1926), p. 416.

The little stone building occupied by the famous General is now a sort of museum, the owner of which lives with his family in the rear part of the house. The "museum" contains a few pistols, a saber or two, some old prints and — a saucer filled with human teeth picked up on the battle field! But, in the main, it is now a store in which souvenirs (made in Japan) and a varied assortment of view cards and booklets on the battle of Gettysburg are sold. In this place, now crowded with babbling chattering, heedless sight-seers, buying post cards, souvenirs, and milk, the silver-haired chief of the Confederate army spent hours and hours of anxious vigil, of deep agony. His men, his officers, his loyal friends, all were falling. His orders, his plans were not being carried out, and yet upon him was the heavy responsibility. Even to the callous tourist it should be possible to visualize the noble, gray-clad figure, pacing up and down the road those nights of uncertainty, awaiting word from Stuart, awaiting word from troops slow in coming up. I wonder how many felt as I did that this place was being desecrated by a souvenir hawker.

Thompson Family Reunion at Ohio Caverns in August, 1955. Courtesy of R. William Bean.

Notes

Part I

1 Robert L. Bloom, *A History of Adams County, Pennsylvania 1700-1990* (Gettysburg, 1992), pp. 5-6.

2 Charles H. Glatfelter and Arthur Weaner, *The Manor Of Maske: Its History And Individual Properties* (Biglerville, 1992), p. 33; Jeffery L. Patterson, *Where Were Lee's Headquarters During The Battle Of Gettysburg, July 1st, 2nd, and 3rd, 1863?* (Not Published, 1982), pp. 5-6. For anyone interested in the early history of the Thompson House, there is no better source than Patterson's very detailed study. A copy of this work can be found in the Lee's Headquarters File at the Adams County Historical Society (hereafter cited as ACHS). Even though the warrant was not issued until 1765, it appears that Robert Stewart may have been a resident as early as 1741.

3 William A. Frassanito, *The Gettysburg Bicentennial Album* (Gettysburg, 1987), pp. 4-5; Bloom, pp. 49-51.

4 Bloom, p. 122; Patterson, pp. 10-11. This road is also commonly referred to as the Cashtown Road or Pike. For the sake of clarity the name Chambersburg Pike will be used throughout this study.

5 Patterson, pp. 3-12.

6 *Ibid.* pp. 14-19. To avoid confusion, the stone house on Seminary Ridge will be referred to as the Thompson House, instead of the Clarkson, or Stevens House, even though Mrs. Thompson may have technically never owned it.

7 Patterson, p. 16.; Tax Records, Borough of Gettysburg, Adams County, Pennsylvania, 1822. The originals of all early Adams County tax records are held in the ACHS.

8 *Compiler*, September 11, 1822.

9 Patterson, pp. 16-17.

10 Charles H. Glatfelter, "Thaddeus Stevens in the Cause of Education: The Gettysburg Years," *Pennsylvania History*, Vol. 60, No. 2 (April 1993), p. 163.

11 Bloom, pp. 125-126; Patterson, p. 17.

12 Patterson, p.17. Section 20 of the railway ran directly across Clarkson's property.

13 Frassanito, *Bicentennial Album*, p. 33. An engraving of Gettysburg in 1843 clearly shows a carriage using the railroad embankment as a road.

14 Patterson, p. 16; Obituary of Thaddeus Stevens Clarkson, *Compiler*, January 23, 1915. T.S. Clarkson served in the Civil War as Adjutant of the 13th Illinois Cavalry, Major of the 3rd Arkansas Cavalry, and as Captain of the 1st Illinois Light Artillery.

15 Appearance and Judgement Docket, Volume T, p. 26. Adams County Courthouse, Gettysburg, Pennsylvania (Hereafter cited as ACC); Patterson, pp. 18-19.

16 Patterson, pp.18-19. An advertisement for the sale of Clarkson's properties appeared in the January 5, 1846, *Adams Sentinel*.

17 Sheriff's Deeds, Insolvent Debtors, Naturalization Docket, January 1842-August 1854, ACC, p. 223. Copy in Thompson Family File at the ACHS.

18 *Registers of Saint John's Evangelical Lutheran Church, Germany Township, Adams County Pennsylvania*, tr. John D. Kilborne (1952), p. 43. Copy in ACHS. There has long been much confusion as to Mary Thompson's maiden name. At times it has been printed as Douglas or Todd, but there seems to be no doubt that she was the daughter of Philip

Long. The baptismal record, the age given at the time of her death, the estate papers of Philip Long, and the tax records of Adams County all lead to this conclusion.

19 Tax Records, Germany Township; Deed Book M, Adams County, ACHS, p. 345; 1820 United States Census, Germany Township, Adams County, Pennsylvania, p. 72. Daniel Sell, born in Pennsylvania, first appears in the Germany Township Tax Records in 1809 as a single man. In 1818 he was still a single man, but in 1819 he was listed as being married. The tax records for 1819 were actually recorded in the fall of 1818, therefore their marriage probably took place in 1818.

20 *Parish Register of Benders Church, Butler Township for the Evangelical Lutheran and Reformed Congregations, 1786-1860*, ACHS, p. 77. Even though she was baptized in Pennsylvania, census records indicate she was born in Maryland.

21 Estate Papers of Daniel Sell, ACHS; *Maryland German Church Records, Volume 7, Saint Mary's Church, Silver Run, Carroll County*, tr. Frederick S. Weiser, p. 34. The exact place or date of death for Daniel Sell has not yet been established, but records indicate he died in Maryland.

22 *The Register of Christ Reformed Church, Littlestown, Pennsylvania, 1747-1871*, tr. Henry James Young, A.B. (1939), p. 44. ACHS.

23 Tax Records, Germany Township, 1826-1827. Again there is no record for the date of this marriage. In 1826, the tax records indicate that Joshua was a single man, and in 1827 he was married. The 1827 Germany Township Tax List was made in the fall of 1826, therefore the marriage probably took place in 1826.

24 In the 1830 U.S. Census Joshua is listed as being between 20 and 30 years of age, giving us a rough idea of his age. One of the questions on the 1880 United States Census asked the person for their parents' birthplace. All of the children of Joshua Thompson I have found in that census answered Pennsylvania.

25 *Registers of Saint John's Evangelical Lutheran Church, Germany Township, Adams County, Pennsylvania, 1763-1900.* tr. John D. Kilbourne (1952), p. 70.

26 Elias Thompson's date of birth was taken from his tombstone which is located in the Fairview Cemetery, West Liberty, Logan County, Ohio.

27 Tax Records, Franklin Township, 1830. Included with the tax records are the lists of poor children for each year. These lists provided clues to Mary Thompson's movements during the 1820s and 30s that could be found nowhere else. Mary's father was named Philip Long, but there was another Philip Long (a brother or an uncle perhaps) who continued to help Mary up into the 1840s. It is not known which Philip Long owned this particular property.

28 1830 United States Census, Franklin Township, Adams County, p. 70. Hannah Phillipina Sell was not living with the family in 1830. This is confirmed by the fact that her name does not appear in the Poor Children's List for Franklin Township in 1831, while both of her sisters' names do. She does appear however in an 1829 "List of Poor Children" for Tyrone Township. Since her older sister "Lizann Sell" [Eliza] also appears on that list, it is possible they were living with relatives.

29 Tax Records, Franklin Township, 1830-1838.

30 *Parish Register of Benders Church, Butler Township for the Evangelical Lutheran and Reformed Congregations, 1786-1860*, pp. 99, 107, 110. ACHS; Appearance and Judgement Docket, Volume R, ACC, p. 946. Susannah Long Thompson was baptized at Benders Church on June 11, 1837, but no date of birth was recorded. At a December 1841 inquest she was said to be "about five or thereabouts." That would place her birth in 1836 or early 1837.

31 Tax Records, Franklin Township, 1831.

32 *Ibid.*, 1837.

33 Estate Papers of Philip Long, ACHS; Tax Records, Franklin Township, 1838-1839. Mary's father died on April 9, 1832. The listing in the 1838 Tax Records is the last known documentation of Joshua Thompson's whereabouts.

34 1840 United States Census, Menallen Township, Adams County, p. 80.

35 Appearance and Judgement Docket, Volume R, ACC, p. 945.

36 *Ibid.*, p. 946.

37 Edward McPherson Papers, Library of Congress. In McPherson's papers is a copy of the proceedings for the sale of the Thompson House in 1889. Transcribed into these proceedings is a letter written by Thaddeus Stevens on March 9, 1850, in which he describes Joshua as Mary's "late husband." At this time there is no other record of Joshua Thompson's death.

38 Thompson Estate Papers, ACHS, Gettysburg, Pennsylvania.

39 The notice that was served Mary Thompson in August 1844 is the first indication that she and her family were living on Seminary Ridge. The 1840 Census indicates that Mary lived in Menallen Township. Therefore she probably moved into Clarkson's stone house in 1841 or 1842, or around the time Ziegler became her children's guardian. It is interesting here to point out that Joshua Thompson, himself, never lived in the house.

40 Sherrif's Deeds, Insolvent Debtors, Naturalization Docket, January 1842-August 1854, ACC, p. 223. Auctioned off were nine different properties totaling over 375 acres, six in Gettysburg and two in Cumberland Township.

41 Thompson Family File, ACHS. Some have suggested that Thaddeus Stevens may have been using the Thompson House as a stop along the famous "Underground Railroad," and some have even advanced the theory that Stevens and Mrs. Thompson were having an affair. Its seems however, that the cause of this speculation is the fact that Stevens somehow managed to purchase the property for only $16 while its value was much greater.

42 *Laws Of The General Assembly Of The Commonwealth Of Pennsylvania, Passed At The Session Of 1848* (Harrisburg, 1848), pp. 536-537.

43 Edward McPherson Papers, Library of Congress. Copy in the Thompson Family File, ACHS. In 1888 this original letter was said to be in the possession of Samuel K. Foulk, Mary's son-in-law.

44 Tax Records, Cumberland Township, 1851-1889. The 1860 Adams County Census also records that Mary Thompson is the owner of the property. It is possible that when Stevens came to Gettysburg in May, 1850 he made some kind of deal with her regarding its ownership. It seems no small coincidence that shortly after this meeting she began to pay taxes on the house and lot in her own name. Since no record of this agreement was ever recorded the property was still legally owned by Thaddeus Stevens at the time of his death, even though he may have given the house to her years earlier. Certainly she would not have paid taxes on a house she did not own.

45 *Minutes of the Board of Directors of the Lutheran Theological Seminary at Gettysburg, Vol. 1 (1826-1862)*, pp. 154, 166, 171, 189. It is possible that the "Miss Thompson" referred to in these minutes is not Mary Thompson, and may be one of the other Miss Thompson's living in town. But considering the date, and the fact that Mary was Lutheran and living close by, it is a safe assumption. In a monograph entitled "The Lutheran Theological Seminary & The Thompson House on Seminary Ridge, Gettysburg, Pa." written by Eugene S. Sickles in 1968, it is mentioned that at the time of the auction

of Clarkson's property, Mrs. Thompson "worked for the Seminary as a cook and a housekeeper." It is not known where Mr. Sickles obtained this information, but a copy of his paper can be found in the Lee's Headquarters file at the ACHS.

46 1850 United States Census, Cumberland Township, Adams County, p. 120. The information provided in the 1850 Census is a mystery. All eight of Mary's children are listed, but all of their ages are wrong, and all of their last names are given as Thompson. This is not possible. Three of the girls, Eliza, Hannah, and Mary Jane, were Sell's. And two of them, Eliza, and Mary Jane were married at the time and not living with Mary. Unfortunately, this mistake by Mary or by the census taker had, up until this book, hidden the fact that she had a first husband.

47 Tax Records, Cumberland Township, 1856.

48 1860 United States Census, Cumberland Township, Adams County, p. 41. Of her eight children in 1860, three were living in Adams County (Hannah, James, and Susannah), two in Ohio (Elias and Mary Jane), one in Missouri (Eliza), and two of them (Margaret and Catherine) cannot be located precisely.

49 *Ibid.*, p. 56. The 1858 Adams County wall map and the 1872 Adams County Atlas both show Mrs. Thompson living directly across the pike from J. Thompson, and several sources (Catherine Foster in a 1904 *Compiler* article for one) indicate that this was Mary's son.

50 *Ibid.*, Gettysburg, p. 210. Samuel Foulk also appears on the 1858 Adams County map living very close to Mrs. Thompson. On the Warren Map, surveyed between 1867-69, this property is shown as the Grimes House, but there is ample evidence that Samuel Foulk and his family lived there at the time of the battle.

Part II

1 Pension Records of John Henry Dustman, National Archives, Washington, D.C. (Hereafter cited as NA); Sheads Family File, ACHS.

2 Pension and Service Records of James Henry Thompson, NA.

3 Samuel P. Bates, *History of Pennsylvania Volunteers: 1861-1865* (Harrisburg, 1870), Vol. 4, pp. 1084-1085.

4 Albertus McCurdy, "Gettysburg: A Boys Experience of the Battle," *Compiler*, June 30, 1909. Copy at ACHS.

5 Robert L. Bloom, "We Never Expected A Battle: The Civilians At Gettysburg, 1863," *Pennsylvania History*, Vol. 55 (October 1988), p. 164.

6 Bloom, *Pennsylvania History*, p. 166; *The War of the Rebellion: A Compilation of the Official Records of the Union and Confederate Armies* (Washington, 1889), Series I, Vol. 27, Part 2, p. 465. (Hereafter cited as *OR*.)

7 Bloom, Civilians, pp. 166-167; *OR* Part 2, p. 465. A copy of this demand is on display at General Lee's Headquarters Museum.

8 Bloom, Civilians, pp. 167-169. *OR* Part 2, p. 465.

9 *OR*, Part 2, p. 298.

10 *Ibid.*, p. 637.

11 Sarah M. Broadhead, *The Diary of a Lady of Gettysburg, Pennsylvania*, Reprinted (Hershey, 1990), p. 11.

12 Daniel Alexander Skelly, *A Boy's Experiences During The Battles of Gettysburg* (Gettysburg, 1932), pp. 10-11.

13 Catherine Foster, "The Story of the Battle: By A Citizen Whose Home Was Pierced By Shells," *Compiler* (June 29, July 6, 1904).

14 Broadhead, p. 12.

15 Casper Henry Dustman, from an unpublished manuscript found in the ACHS, n.d.

Part III

1 Robert K. Beecham, *The Pivotal Battle of the Civil War* (Chicago, 1911), p. 78.
2 *Ibid.*
3 Rufus R. Dawes, *Service with the Sixth Wisconsin Volunteers* (Marietta, Ohio), p. 175.
4 *OR*, Part 1, pp. 347, 350. Abner Doubleday, *Chancellorsville and Gettysburg* (New York, 1886), p. 147. With the death of John Reynolds, Doubleday had assumed command of the Union First Army Corps.
5 Doubleday, p. 147.
6 *A Diary of Battle: The Personal Journals of Colonel Charles S. Wainwright, 1861-1865*, ed. Allen Nevins (New York, 1962), p. 235.
7 Beecham, p. 80. Cooper's Battery B, 1st Pennsylvania Light Artillery, actually had four guns present during the battle, but only three were in action along Seminary Ridge. One piece, an "axle having broken from recoil at the first few shots" earlier in the day, was not engaged. See *OR*, Part 1, p. 365.
8 *OR*, Part 1, p. 336.
9 Frank E. Foster, from an affidavit, dated July 12, 1925, which is on display at General Lee's Headquarters Museum and Gift Shop. There seems to be very little doubt that this document is authentic. According to the compiled Service and Pension Records at the National Archives, Frank Foster was indeed a member of Co. H, 143rd Pennsylvania, and was present at the battle. He died in Long Beach, California, on September 6, 1927.
10 John Musser, "The Civil War Letters of Lt. Col. John Musser, 143rd P.V.I.," *Ronald D. Boyer Collection*, United States Army Military History Institute (USAMHI) Carlisle, Pennsylvania, December 10, 1863.
11 James Stewart, "Battery B, Fourth United States Artillery At Gettysburg." *MOLLUS-OH*, Vol.4, p. 185.
12 Beecham, pp. 80-81.
13 Dawes, p. 175.
14 Augustus Buell, "The Story of a Cannoneer," *National Tribune*, October 10, 1889, through April 3, 1890. In 1890 it was also published by the *National Tribune* in the form of a paperback book.
15 Most modern historians have taken it for granted that Buell was a member of the battery and most books dealing with the first day's battle use his account as a primary source. Edwin Coddington, who wrote The *Gettysburg Campaign: A Study in Command* (New York, 1968), seems to be the exception to the rule.
16 Milton W. Hamilton, "Augustus Buell, Fraudulent Historian," *Pennsylvania Magazine of History and Biography*, 80 (October 1956), pp. 478-492; Silas Felton, "Pursuing the Elusive 'cannoneer,'" *Gettysburg Magazine* No. 9 (July 1993), pp. 33-39; Pension Records of Augustus Buell, NA; Muster Rolls of the 4th United States Light Artillery, 1861-1865, NA. In reading Buell's obituary it is interesting to note that the 4th U.S. was not the only regiment that he claimed to be a member of. However, no Augustus Buell shows up on the muster rolls for Battery B, 4th United States Artillery for any period during the Civil War. But probably the most compelling evidence is found in his pension record on file at the National Archives. At the time of Buell's death, his wife was not sure what unit he had served in, and because of his many claims, she, as well as the pensioners were quite confused.
17 Augustus Buell, *The Cannoneer: Story of A Private Soldier*, published by the *National Tribune* (Washington, D. C., 1890), pp. 67-70.

18 James Stewart, *National Tribune*, November 21, and December 26, 1889. James Stewart was born on May 18, 1826, in Edinburgh, Scotland. He came to America in 1844, enlisted in Battery B, 4th U. S. Artillery in 1851, and served until March 20, 1879 in the regular army. He died at Fort Thomas, Kentucky, on April 19, 1905, and is now buried in Arlington National Cemetery.

19 During a visit to the Gettysburg Battlefield in 1882 Scales stated that "the fire of Battery B was the most destructive he had known in the war." Dawes, p. 175.

20 *OR*, Part 2, p. 670.

21 *Ibid.*, p. 671.

22 *Histories of the Several Regiments and Battalions from North Carolina in the Great War*, ed. Walter Clark (Raleigh, 1901), Vol. 1, p. 698.

23 *Ibid.*, Vol. 2, p. 586. Unfortunately for Scales' Brigade it would not be the last time they would be repulsed. Just two days later this brigade would be part of the attacking force in the infamous "Pickett's Charge."

24 *Pennsylvania at Gettysburg: Ceremonies at the Dedication of the Monuments Erected by the Commonwealth of Pennsylvania to Mark the Positions of the Pennsylvania Commands Engaged in the Battle*, ed. John P. Nicholson (Harrisburg, 1904), Vol. 2, pp. 898-899. Hereafter referred to as *PA*.

25 Beecham, p. 80.

26 *Ibid.*, p. 81

Part IV

1 Beecham, pp. 86-89.

2 *Ibid.*, pp. 88-89.

3 J.F.J. Caldwell, *The History Of A Brigade Of South Carolinians, Known First As "Gregg's" And Subsequently As "McGowan's Brigade"* (Philadelphia, 1866), p. 97.

4 *OR*, Part 2, p. 661.

5 Caldwell, p. 97.

6 *OR*, Part 2, p.662.

7 Varina Davis Brown, *A Colonel At Gettysburg And Spotsylvania* (Columbia, 1931), pp. 79-80. Varina Brown was the daughter of Colonel Brown, and joined her father on many trips to the Gettysburg Battlefield. This book is one of the best ever written dealing with the first day's battle.

8 Brown, p. 80. *OR*, Part 2, p. 662.

9 Brown, p. 80.

10 *PA*, Vol. 2, p. 763.

11 *Ibid.*

12 Caldwell, p. 98.

13 *OR*, Part 1, p. 251.

14 Nevins, p. 237.

15 *Ibid.*

16 Dawes, p. 176. After the war, it became almost a sport among Northern writers to blame the soldiers of the Eleventh Corps for the defeat of the First Corps. These accounts, however, ignore the fact that Perrin's Brigade had captured the Seminary, and this was the reason Doubleday was calling for a retreat.

17 Musser Letters, September 15, 1863.

18 Dawes, p.176.

19 Stewart, p. 187.

20 George Grant, "The First Army Corps On the First Day At Gettysburg," *MOLLUS-MINN*, Vol. 5, p. 52.

21 Stewart, p. 188.

22 Musser Letters, December 10, 1863.

23 Unidentified author, *Wake Forest Student* (April 1894), p. 451.

24 Clark, Vol.1, p. 719.

25 Nevins, p. 236.

26 Clark, Vol. 1, p. 719. The comment was made by Colonel Risden Tyler Bennett of the 14th North Carolina.

27 *OR*, Part 1, p. 280.

28 *Robert Brake Collection*, USAMHI, Box 12, 7th Wisconsin File. Letter written July 30, 1863.

29 *Ibid.*, Letter dated July 11, 1863.

30 *OR*, Part 2, p.582. The area that Doles' Brigade crossed on their advance toward the retreating Northern soldiers is not part of the Gettysburg National Military Park and is now owned by the Gettysburg College, and as a result has dramatically changed.

31 Grant, pp. 52-53.

32 Wilbur Judd, *Herkimer County Journal*, July 25, 1863.

33 *Three Years With Company K*, ed. Arthur A. Kent, (London, 1976), p. 182.

34 *The Road to Richmond: The Civil War Memoirs of Maj. Abner R. Small Of The 16th Maine Vols.; With His Diary As A Prisoner Of War*, ed. Harold Adams Small (Berkley, 1939), pp. 101-102.

35 *Maine At Gettysburg: Report of the Maine Commissioners Prepared by the Executive Committee* (Portland, 1898), p. 44.

36 Francis Wiggin, "The Sixteenth Maine Regiment At Gettysburg," *MOLLUS-MA*, Vol. 4, p. 159.

37 George D. Bisbee, "Three Years A Volunteer," *MOLLUS-ME* (1910), p. 10.

38 *OR*, Part 2, p. 575.

39 *Ibid.*, Part 1, p. 173. Until recently this railroad cut was included in the boundary of the Gettysburg National Military Park and could be visited by any American citizen. In 1991 however, a 7.5 acre tract of land, which included part of the cut, was transferred by Park officials to the Gettysburg College, who in turn excavated the portion of the ridge where this fighting occurred. To the outrage of historians, this injustice has continued to be defended by Park Service and College officials.

40 *Ibid.*, Part 2, p. 573. The accounts of Daniel's Brigade taking prisoners are of particular importance because they indicate that the brigade stopped at the railroad cut and spent the night nearby. This brigade did not enter the town on July 1st, and therefore the hundreds of prisoners they claim to have taken must have been captured near the railroad cut, and not in the town as many have suggested.

41 *New York Monuments Commission for the Battlefields of Gettysburg and Chattanooga. Final Report on the Battlefield of Gettysburg*, ed. William F. Fox (Albany, 1900), Vol. 2, p. 757.

42 For an in depth study of the Union and Confederate losses during the battle see *Regimental Strengths and Losses at Gettysburg* by John W. Busey and David G. Martin (Hightstown, 1986).

Part V

1 *Brake Collection*, Box 11, 150th Pennsylvania File.

2 Musser Letters, September 15, 1863.

3   Stewart, pp. 186-187.

4   *Potter Journal*, September, 18, 1879. This is an account by a veteran of the 53rd Pennsylvania who was returning to the field to visit the scene of the battle. On his tour he spoke with Casper Henry Dustman.

5   Dustman, ACHS.

6   Gregory A. Coco, *A Vast Sea Of Misery* (Gettysburg, 1988), p. 11. It is interesting to note that in Dustman's claim to the government after the war for damages to his property, he does not mention his house being used as a hospital. He was only concerned with the fact that when the Rebels "retreated they took from his barn...his new carriage," which he had just purchased a short time before. Interestingly enough, one of his witnesses was Mary Thompson's daughter, Hannah Foulk.   Her affidavit was dated October 22, 1868. "About a week before the battle of Gettysburg, I saw Mr. Dustman take his carriage to his barn and I saw it in his barn. After the battle I was at his barn and the carriage was not there. I asked him where his carriage was. He told me it had been taken by the Rebels. Hannah P. Foulk"

7   Foster, *Compiler*. The full account given by Catherine Foster in the 1904 *Compiler* concerning James Thompson's family is as follows: "Her [Mary's] son and family, consisting of wife and two children, the younger but one day old, also remained in their house until the afternoon when it was filled with wounded and dying men of the 1st Corps, then they started, carrying their children. They were passed through the rebel lines to the rear and they all survived to tell the tale."

Another account of James Thompson's family during the battle was given by James' second wife, Elizabeth, in 1911, and appears in his Pension Records at the National Archives. "James H. Thompson's first wife and mother of [four of] his children was Mary [Jane] Arent. She died during the war. James H. Thompson was in the Army and the Rebels came and drove his wife out of his house, she having been confined with a child only about three days before, and she walked to her Mother's, distance five miles, and took cold and died."

A third account of James H. Thompson is given in a letter by his daughter, Ella N. Murphy in 1908, and also appears in Thompson's Pension Records. "I think his home was in Gettesburg, Pa time of the Gettesburg battle was fought. His elisment the first time run out just before the battle. He went home to see his wife, my mother. General Lee had his headquarters in part of his mothers house so they got after him and he had to leave and he went back and relisted and staied out till the close of the War."

James H. Thompson was indeed serving in the Union army at the time of the battle. He served in Co. H 165th Pennsylvania, and could not have possibly been present in Gettysburg until a couple of weeks after the battle. His first wife was Mary Jane Arendt, and at the time of the battle they had a four year old son, Elias F. Thompson. Mary Jane did not die shortly after the battle, but on March 7, 1869. The fact that two independent sources suggested that she gave birth to another child just prior to the battle has always puzzled the author. Would not such an amazing occurance have been noted long ago by some other historian? Considering that there is no mention of this child in the 1870 census, and that no death for this child was ever recorded in the local newspapers, makes this story hard to believe. But research conducted by the author just weeks prior to publication of this book has revealed some startling new information.

Burial records of the Evergreen Cemetery record that a small child is buried with Mary Jane Arendt Thompson in her unmarked grave (Lot 253, Section G). The child died of "inflamation of [the] lungs" on March 8, 1864, and was named Jane Meade Thompson. The burial permit records that the child was "eight months & 9 days old," making her date of birth June 30, 1863. To the best knowledge of the author this would make Jane the youngest resident of Gettysburg at the time of the battle. It is probably no small coincidence that her middle name was "Meade." Around the year 1872 James remarried Elizabeth Routson Witmore, the widow of Benjamin Witmore who had died during the war. Shortly after their marriage they moved west and eventually settled in Springhill, Champaign County, Ohio (see Appendix).

8   Records Relating to Civil War Border Claims. Damage Claims Applications Submitted Under Act passed 1863-1865, Adams County, Samuel Foulk, File No. 3360, Copy on microfilm at ACHS; Obituary of Annie M. Foulk, *Compiler*, May 2, 1931. Elias Sheads and Casper Henry Dustman were both witnesses to Foulk's claim.

In Annie Foulk's obituary it mentioned that "the family lived on Buford Ave. [Chambersburg Pike] in the house known as 'the White Hospital' during the Battle of Gettysburg." Annie was six years of age at the time of the battle. There is also a letter written by Percy Samuel Eichelberger, a grandson of Hannah Foulk, that talks of the house being used as a hospital. The letter was written on July 14, 1953, on Larson's Cottage Court stationery. It is now in the possession of the author.

"Foulk[s] five children kept in [the] cellar [during the battle]. My mother [Sallie] was the baby, their house was used as a hospital, with [Samuel] Foulk bringing in the wounded. ...Mrs. Thompson had...[a] son-in-law [who was] a officer in [the] Southern Army in MO. Lee wanted to pay in Confederate money, but Mrs. Thompson said he was a guest and she didn't take money from guests. ...Mrs. Thompson's daughter who lived down [the] street [Hannah] would not let her return to [her] house the 2nd day." Mary did, in fact, have a son-in-law that lived in Missouri at the time of the Civil War. His name was Henry Long and he was married to Mary's eldest daughter, Eliza. They were married in the 1850s and moved west shortly before the outbreak of the Civil War. Henry was born in Adams County, and while it seemed unusual that he served in the Confederate Army, according to service records at the National Archives there were three Henry Longs that served in the Confederate Army from Missouri. At the present time, it is not known for certain whether he was one of them.

9   Sheads Family File, ACHS; Coco, p. 10. A book in itself could be written on the Sheads House and the events that occurred around it.

10 Foster, *Compiler; Battle of Gettysburg, A Citizen's Eyewitness Account by Catherine Mary White Foster*, ed. David A. Murdoch (Pittsburgh, 1994), p.6. Both of the Foster accounts are very similar with variations in only a few paragraphs. The quote given here is a combination of the two accounts.

11 Patterson, p. 28. In a monograph written by Eugene Sickles in 1968 (copy in ACHS), there is another description of Mary's role in comforting the wounded.

"When the battle broke on McPherson's Ridge on July 1, Mrs. Thompson went to the Seminary, where she remained in the basement and done everything she could, despite the holocaust going on around her, to assist the wounded as they were brought in from the fields. Late in the evening, she witnessed the headlong rush of Perrin's victorious South Carolinians as they passed the Seminary buildings on the way to the town....She spent the best part of the second and third days at the Seminary building, where she was sickened by the sight of so many wounded and horribly mangled men, both blue and gray."

Unfortunately, it is unknown where Sickles obtained the information for his monograph. See note #18 of this section for an explanation.

12 James Power Smith, "General Lee at Gettysburg," *Southern Historical Society Papers*, Vol. 33 (1905), pp. 140-141.

13 William A. Frassanito, *Gettysburg: A Journey In Time* (New York, 1975), p. 73.

14 Affidavit in collection of General Lee's Headquarters Museum, dated July 2, 1913. Martin V. Gander does indeed show up on the muster rolls of Company C, 39th Virginia Battalion of Cavalry. These records at the National Archives also indicate that he enlisted at Luray, Virginia. On its muster rolls, the 39th Virginia Battalion is described as "Scouts, Guides, and Couriers."

15 *An Aide-De-Camp Of Lee*, ed. Frederick Maurice (Boston, 1927), p. 233. Charles Marshall's manuscript, around which Maurice's book was constructed, was written in the 1870s. This was much earlier than when the controversy began over whether Lee did or did not use the stone house as his headquarters. Charles Marshall more than any other person was in a position to know where Lee spent the night.

16 John D. Imboden, "Lee At Gettysburg," *Galaxy Magazine*, Vol. 1871, p. 507.

17 1860 Census, Cumberland Township, p. 41. This suggestion was offered by Licensed Battlefield Guide Eugene Sickels in a monograph written on Lee's Headquarters in 1968 entitled *The Lutheran Theological Seminary & The Thompson House on Seminary Ridge, Gettysburg, PA*. A copy of this is in the Lee's Headquarters File at the ACHS.

18 Michael Jacobs, "Later Rambles Over the Field of Gettysburg," *The United States Service Magazine*, Vol. 1, (New York, 1864), p. 66; Patterson, p. 37.

Another account of Lee and his staff using the Thompson House during the battle appears in the monograph of the Thompson House written by Eugene Sickles in 1968 (ACHS).

After the first day's battle west of town subsided, and while the Confederates were moving up their artillery and consolidating their positions atop the ridge, Mrs. Thompson returned [from the Seminary] unmolested to her bullet-riddled and shell-ripped home, to find General Robert E. Lee, General A.P. Hill, General James Longstreet, General William Pendleton, and General James Lane, along with Colonels [Charles] Marshall, Cole, and [James L.] Corley of Lee's staff, having dismounted from their horses in the road in front of the house and standing in a group inside the fence. She introduced herself, after which Colonel Cole asked her if she could be hired to provide the group with a hot meal. She readily assented, and went inside to prepare it, while a detail of Confederate soldiers brought flour and beans in from the wagons, and drew water from the well for her. She also offered the use of the vacant side of the house to the group. Colonel Marshall thanked her, and the soldiers set about to establish a place for administrative work there, carrying in trunks and a desk.

Her kitchen table, a rather small festive board for such a large group, was carried into the yard, where the meal was served under the trees. General Lee thanked her personally for her kindness, complimented her on the meal's result, and instructed Colonel Marshall to see to it that she was adequately rewarded. Three tents were erected by the soldiers on the opposite side of the pike, one of which was intended for General Lee's use, while the staff officers busied themselves in the temporary headquarters. Mrs. Thompson served breakfast to a few of the staff officers on the morning of the second day, but she did not see any of the high command officers after that, although the administrative office remained in the vacant section of her house until the time of the retreat.

I feel that a note of explanation should be given here on the use of this document in this book. The monograph in question, *The Lutheran Theological Seminary & The*

Thompson House on Seminary Ridge, Gettysburg, PA, was written by Licensed Battlefield Guide Eugene S. Sickles on September 1, 1968. It is five typed pages in length, and is very detailed in its content. Unfortunately, it is not known where the documentation for the information in his paper was obtained. To make matters worse, the monograph is marred with factual errors which are easily discredited. Being a battlefield guide, myself, the author has first-hand knowledge of how "old guide stories" have passed down from generation to generation and can take on a life of their own. Because of few accounts that exist concerning Mrs. Thompson during the battle, and because of the interesting nature of the account, I have chosen to include some of Sickles' stories in my footnotes, but must point out that I, myself, question the origin of his monograph.

Eugene Sickles, born in Chillicothe, OH was a veteran of World War II, and a respected citizen in Gettysburg for many years. He was best known as an artist who "painted hundreds of signs, and made numerous dioramas and models of cannons, soldiers, horses, etc. for local museums." He died on March 30, 1975 (see Obituary, Gettysburg *Times*, March 31, 1975), and some of his work is still on display at many of Gettysburg's attractions.

19 Lee's Headquarters File, ACHS. A transcript of this letter was made in June 1949, and a copy somehow managed to make it into the files of the ACHS. It is not known where the original is located, but their is little doubt as to its authenticity. A clipping from an early relic dealer's catalogue also gives a transcription of part of the letter. It is not known what year the letter was sold, but it was valued at only $12.50.

20 Martin V. Gander, Affidavit.

21 *OR*, Part 2, p. 604.

22 *Ibid.*, p. 568.

23 *Ibid.*, p. 604.

24 *Ibid.*, p. 603. As a result of the battle of July 1st, and of Union counterbattery fire on July 2nd and 3rd, many of the buildings along Seminary Ridge were struck by artillery shells meant for the enemy. The Schmucker House, the Seminary building, the Sheads House, and the Dustman Barn were all hit with shells during these bombardments. The Schmucker House and the Sheads House still have shells imbedded in them today.

25 Broadhead, p. 15.

26 This line of wooden breastworks is shown on all contemporary maps of the battlefield and it also appears in a famous Mathew Brady photograph showing three Confederate prisoners on Seminary Ridge. See Frassanito, *Journey*, pp. 70-71.

27 *OR*, Part 2, p. 604.

28 Jacobs, p. 66.

29 Abdel Ross Wentz, *Gettysburg Lutheran Theological Seminary*, (Harrisburg, 1965), Vol. 1, p. 217.

30 *Ibid.*, pp. 212-213.

31 Claims file, Harriet B. Krauth, ACHS. The Reverend Doctor Charles Philip Krauth died on May 30, 1867. The claim was being filed by his widow. Hannah P. Foulk's affidavit was dated November 28, 1868. Living so close, the Thompson's and Foulk's seem to have had a close association with the Lutheran Seminary. Hannah's son, David Foulk, graduated from the Seminary in 1873.

32 Broadhead, p. 23.

33 Frassanito, *Journey*, pp. 37-38; Patterson, p. 36.

34 "Reminiscences of Gettysburg," *Harper's Weekly*, Vol. 7, no. 347 (August 22, 1863), p. 534.

Part VI

1   "The Gettysburgh Celebration," New York *Times*, November 21, 1863.
2   Mrs. Edmund A. Souder, *Leaves from the Battlefield of Gettysburg* (Philadelphia, 1864), p. 137.
3   *Reflections on the Battle of Gettysburg*, ed. Ralph S. Shay (Lebanon County Historical Society, 1963), p. 300-301.
4   "The American Necropolis," New York *Herald*, November 20, 1863.
5   "The Gettysburg Ceremonies," New York *Daily Tribune*, November 21, 1863.
6   Note on display at General Lee's Headquarters Museum. Apparently the table was purchased by Clyde Daley sometime before February 1923, the date of Alice Foulk's death, and has been on display ever since. It must be mentioned that Alice herself did not write the note that is on display as her name (Folk) is spelled incorrectly. It was verbal information given by her.
7   As mentioned in Footnote No. 7, Part V of this book, there are conflicting accounts of Mary Arendt Thompson's whereabouts during the battle. It must also be mentioned at this point that it is possible the person who wrote the note did not know Joshua was Mary's husband and mistakenly wrote Mrs. James Thompson. Other people have also made this mistake, see Patterson p. 24.
8   1860 Census, Gettysburg, p. 210.
9   Ezra K. Warner, *Generals in Blue* (Baton Rouge, 1965), pp. 217-218.
10 "As to Lee's Headquarters," *Compiler*, April 20, 1910.
11 *Isometric Map of the Gettysburg Battlefield*, 1863.
12 *Elliotts' Map of the Battlefield of Gettysburg* (Philadelphia, 1864); *Report of the Select Committee Relative to the Soldiers' National Cemetery* (Harrisburg, 1864), frontpiece. Part of these breastworks can still be seen along the crest of Oak Ridge just north of the Thompson House. About 30 yards of these original breastworks were recently removed by the Gettysburg College.
13 From a letter written on July 22, 1866, from Thaddeus Stevens to John H. McClellan. The original is in private hands. A copy is in the Thompson Family File at the ACHS.
14 Gettysburg *Star and Sentinel*, June 4, 1873; Patterson, p. 29.
15 McPherson Papers, Library of Congress; Patterson, p. 29; *Compiler*, December 18, 1888.
16 Obituary of Philip Hennig, *Compiler*, March 16, 1918; Hennig Family File, ACHS.
17 McPherson Papers, Library of Congress.
18 *Ibid.*
19 *Ibid.*
20 *Ibid.* The five remaining Thompson children were recorded as: "1- James Henry Thompson of Champaign County, Ohio, P.O. West Liberty, 2- Elias Thompson of Same Place, 3- Margaret Isabella Thompson, intermarried with —— Barnett of Kansas, 4- Susan Thompson, intermarried with Napoleon Sowers of Penna, 5- Sarah Thompson, now widow of —— Yohn of Gettysburg, Penna."
21 In the year 1900 the only Southern monuments on the field were the Armistead marker at the Angle, the 2nd Maryland regimental monument on Culp's Hill, and the 2nd Maryland advanced position marker, also on Culp's Hill. All three of these monuments were erected by citizens of Maryland, which technically, was not a Southern state.
22 Postcards really did not become popular until the early 20th century. Today Lee's Headquarters postcards can easily be found at local flea markets.
23 Holman D. Waldron, *With Pen and Camera on the Field of Gettysburg in War and Peace* (Portland, 1898).

24 Benson Lossing, *Pictorial History of the Civil War in the United States of America* (Hartford, 1868), Vol. III, p. 64. The earliest account of a postwar visit to the Thompson House that the author has been able to uncover was located in a newspaper article written by a man named Castine on June 14, 1865. The article described his journey over the Gettysburg Battlefield. A clipping of this article can be found on p. 60 of Edward McPherson's Battle of Gettysburg Scrapbook, Edward McPherson Papers, Library of Congress.

"Due west from the College building, on the Chambersburg Pike, is a small one-story stone house. The headquarters of Lee during the fight, though he went back to the mountain always at night to rest and sleep."

25 *Ibid.*
26 *Potter Journal*, September 18, 1879.
27 1860 Census, Gettysburg, p. 162.
28 John D. Vanderslice, *Gettysburg, Then and Now* (Gettysburg, 1899), pp. 137, 140.

Part VII

1 "Lee's Headquarters Destroyed," *Compiler*, September 1, 1896. It does not appear that Philip Hennig ever lived in the house on Seminary Ridge, and just rented it out. Another resident of the house under his ownership was Israel Lentz. His son Albert, "who lived a number of years in Lee's Headquarters" has the distinction of being the first Adams Countian killed in the First World War. He is buried in the National Cemetery, and the American Legion in Gettysburg is named after him. See *Compiler*, May 11, 1918.

2 *Ibid.*
3 *Compiler*, June 5, 1907; 1900 United States Census, Adams County, Gettysburg, p.101. Emma Feister, a widowed mother of seven children, pleaded guilty in Adams County Court on August 26, 1907. Her sentence was suspended.
4 "Where Were General Lee's Headquarters at Gettysburg," *Compiler*, March 30, 1910.
5 *The Pennsylvania College Book 1832-1882* (Philadelphia, 1882), ed. E. S. Bridinbaugh, p. 309; Philip Columbus Croll was indeed a student at the College as Moyer indicates, therefore the date of Moyer's visit to Gettysburg is correct. See Patterson, p. 54.
6 *Compiler*, March 30, 1910.
7 Gettysburg *Star and Sentinel*, June 4, 1873; Estate Papers of Mary Thompson, ACHS. Since we know the date of Moyer's visit can be documented by Philip Croll's enrollment at the college, and considering the fact that no other "old lady" lived with Mary in the Thompson House, Moyer's statements must not be altogether truthful.
8 "More as to Lee's Headquarters," *Compiler*, July 20, 1910.
9 *Ibid.*
10 *The Bachelder Papers*, tr. David L. and Audrey J. Ladd, (Morningside, 1994), Vol. 1, pp. 9-14. The bulk of Bachelder Papers are held at the New Hampshire Historical Society.
11 "Gen. Lee's Headquarters," *Compiler*, August 3, 1910.
12 Henry S. Moyer, *General Lee's Headquarters at Gettysburg, Penna.* (Allentown, 1911), 4 pp. The 1900 Census indicates Moyer was born in Pennsylvania in October 1851. At that time he was single, and lived with his sister's family in Allentown.
13 Affidavit in collection of Lee's Headquarters Museum.
14 Service Records of Martin V. Gander, NA.
15 Affidavit in collection of Lee's Headquarters Museum. It is possible that the identity of this individual may still be ascertained.
16 Affidavit in collection of Lee's Headquarters Museum.

17 Henry Kyd Douglas, *I Rode with Stonewall* (Chapel Hill, 1940), p. 358. Douglas died in December 1903. There is much speculation regarding these documents. The most likely scenario is that the Douglas affidavit, dated three weeks later from Hagerstown, Maryland, is a fake. Altogether there are five affidavits in the museum's collection: the three Confederate documents, Frank Foster's account of the 143rd PA, and Alice Foulk's account of the table.

18 "Lee's Servant Here on Friday," Gettysburg *Times*, June 9, 1917.

19 *Ibid.*

20 Patterson, p. 60; *Reports G.N.M.P. 1912-21 Volume 2, Annual Report of the Gettysburg National Park Commission, June 30, 1919*, pp. 2-3.

21 It is not positively known that the quote on the monument was taken directly from Moyer's booklet. It is possible that the Park had access to the same information Moyer did, and used it independently of his study.

22 *Compiler*, March 16, 1918; Patterson, p. 31.

23 Undated Gettysburg newspaper clipping from scrapbook at Lee's Headquarters Museum.

24 1920 Census, Gettysburg, p.168; Interview with Andrew M. and Allen A. Larson, December 28, 1994; Obituary of Samuel E. Trimmer, *Compiler*, March 4, 1922.

25 It is not known exactly who gathered together the relics that now make up the museum's collection. The Larson brothers, who owned the museum for many years, believe that it was Samuel Trimmer, who was very wealthy, owning a chain of five and ten cent stores. When his daughter married Clyde Daley, the manager of his Gettysburg store, they say Trimmer bought Lee's Headquarters as a present for them. It is not known what part, if any, Hennig played in collecting artifacts, but some of the documents do predate Daley's ownership. Regardless of their origin, today the artifacts on display at Lee's Headquarters Museum have been on continuous display longer than any other private collection in Gettysburg.

26 Larson Interview; Obituary of Eric F. Larson, Gettysburg *Times*, October 22, 1968.

27 Larson Interview; Patterson p. 31.

28 Again, in 1900 those three monuments would be the 2nd Maryland Infantry monument on Culp's Hill, its advance position marker, and the Armistead marker at the Angle.

Index

About the Author

Timothy H. Smith is employed as a licensed battlefield guide and instructor for the Gettysburg Elderhostel. He acts as a volunteer reference historian at the Adams County Historical Society and occasionally teaches non-credit classes on the battle and local history at local community colleges. He is a frequent lecturer at Civil War seminars and round table meetings. He has written numerous articles concerning the battle and is the author of *John Burns, The Hero of Gettysburg* and the co-author of *Devil's Den, A History and Guide*. He lives in Gettysburg with his wife and son.

THOMAS PUBLICATIONS publishes books about the American Colonial era, the Revolutionary War, the Civil War, and other important topics. For a complete list of titles, please visit our website at:

www.thomaspublications.com

Or write to:

THOMAS PUBLICATIONS
P.O. Box 3031
Gettysburg, PA 17325